WHO WILL SPEAK
FOR AMERICA?

WHO WILL SPEAK FOR AMERICA?

SAMIRA AHMED · CHARLIE JANE ANDERS · CYNTHIA ARRIEU-KING · CYNTHIA ATKINS · HERMAN BEAVERS · JERICHO BROWN · ADRIENNE CELT · RENE DENFELD · LINH DINH · VERONICA SCOTT ESPOSITO · SARAH ROSE ETTER · MELISSA FEBOS · LIANA FINCK · GANZEER · NANCY HIGHTOWER · BASSEY IKPI · MOHJA KAHF · KEN KALFUS · JOY LADIN · ANA-MAURINE LARA · CARMEN MARIA MACHADO · JUAN MARTINEZ · AIREA D. MATTHEWS · DIANE MCKINNEY-WHETSTONE · LYNN MELNICK · SAM J. MILLER · LIZ MOORE · EILEEN MYLES · SANDRA NEWMAN · ALICE NOTLEY · CYNTHIA DEWI OKA · TAHNEER OKSMAN · MALKA OLDER · CRAIG SANTOS PEREZ · MARC ANTHONY RICHARDSON · CARLOS JOSÉ PÉREZ SÁMANO · JEFFREY STOCKBRIDGE · MADELEINE THIEN · EDWIN TORRES · KC TROMMER · ADAM VINES · FRAN WILDE

Edited by Stephanie Feldman *and* Nathaniel Popkin

TEMPLE UNIVERSITY PRESS 　 T 　 *Philadelphia · Rome · Tokyo*

TEMPLE UNIVERSITY PRESS
Philadelphia, Pennsylvania 19122
www.temple.edu/tempress

Copyright © 2018 by Temple University—Of The Commonwealth System
   of Higher Education
All rights reserved
Published 2018

Design by Kate Nichols

Cataloging-in-Publication data is on file with the Library of Congress.

ISBN 978-1-4399-1624-7 (paper)
ISBN 978-1-4399-1625-4 (ebook)

♾ The paper used in this publication meets the requirements of the American National
Standard for Information Sciences—Permanence of Paper for Printed Library Materials,
ANSI Z39.48-1992

Printed in the United States of America

9 8 7 6 5 4 3 2 1

To those unwilling to forfeit their voices, no matter the risk

CONTENTS

To Ourselves

To Our Americas

PART II: SPEAKING FOR AMERICA

For the Nation

For the Future

ACKNOWLEDGMENTS

We thank PEN America, Erin Belieu, and the organizers of Writers Resist; Alicia Askenase, Elisabeth Jaquette, Elizabeth Scanlon, and Eric Smith for their advice; Leah Paulos; Sara Cohen, for encouraging us to create this book and then bringing it to Temple University Press, and her colleagues Nikki Miller, Kate Nichols, Ann-Marie Anderson, Gary Kramer, Irene Imperio Kull, and David Wilson; Rebecca Logan; Paula Weiss; and Barbara Jordan, whose 1976 speech inspired the construction of this anthology. We are honored to donate proceeds from this book to the Southern Poverty Law Center, which is dedicated to fighting hate and bigotry and to seeking justice for the most vulnerable members of our society. We are grateful to the contributors for their time, enthusiasm, and words and to our families for their support.

WHO WILL SPEAK
FOR AMERICA?

INTRODUCTION

IN SEARCH OF OUR FUTURE

Stephanie Feldman and Nathaniel Popkin

I n the bicentennial year of the Declaration of Independence, U.S. Representative Barbara Jordan, a veteran of the civil rights movement, gave the first address by a black woman to the Democratic National Convention in New York City. She opened her speech by describing American sentiment in the aftermath of Watergate and the Vietnam War: "Many fear the future. Many are distrustful of their leaders, and believe that their voices are never heard. Many seek only to satisfy their private work." Jordan wondered what would become of American civic life and worried that it would dissolve into perpetual conflict, "city against suburb, region against region, individual against individual." "If that happens," she asked, "who then will speak for America?"[1]

Forty years later, in the immediate wake of the 2016 election of Donald J. Trump as president of the United States, many of us recognized Jordan's assessment of the national mood. Trump had embraced white supremacist supporters and run a divisive, fear-mongering campaign that openly targeted marginalized communities, including Latin American immigrants, Muslims, and people with disabilities. The new vice president, Mike Pence, the former governor of Indiana, had a disturbing record of Christian extremism and radical homophobia. Both men displayed antipathy toward science and scholarly inquiry. Would their administration continue this assault, through both policy and rhetoric? Our home city, Philadelphia, which had rebounded after nearly sixty years of population decline, felt particularly vulnerable. Immigrants, people of color, and sexual minorities are central to the city's cultural vibrancy. Diversity, an object of Trump's scorn, is a public good. Moreover, higher education, medical science, and biotechnology fuel the city's economy. What if the new administration and its allies in the Republican Congress followed through on their threats?

As writers, we sensed still another danger: Trump had targeted—and, in his electoral triumph, damaged—elements of civil life long protected by our social contract, such as respect for the constitutional balance of power and recognition of the essential role of the media in a free society. The Trump campaign jeopardized people's lives and well-being, but it also revealed the vulnerability of American political institutions. His campaign's proclivity for lies—or, as his spokesperson would later say, "alternative facts"—threatened the function of democracy itself. Were we facing a tyranny of lies? For writers, this felt like an urgent personal challenge. What is the place of writers when the media is under threat and when language itself is abused and turned into a weapon?

A new vocabulary emerged. Activists, both experienced and novice, began to speak about normalization and kleptocracy, and Trump's opponents coalesced around the idea of resistance, asking ourselves what issues we would prioritize and what skills we might bring to the new political movement. Writers flocked to the grassroots plan for a Writers Resist campaign and organized over one hundred literary protests—rallies for free expression and democracy—on January 15, 2017, the weekend before Trump's inauguration.

While the flagship protest in New York City was cosponsored by PEN America, events elsewhere were conceived and organized locally. In Philadelphia, we, along with poet Alicia Askenase, gathered our community on Independence Mall, where foundational American protests occurred. Poet Erin Belieu, founder of Writers Resist (now Write Our Democracy), encouraged each group to craft an event that attended to local concerns. We wanted Philadelphia's Writers Resist protest to reflect the city's present-day diversity, as well as its political history.

As organizers, we soon realized that the act of protest was an act of imagination. There was an inherent tension in resisting an administration that had yet to take office. We were resisting Trump's campaign practices and promises, yes, but the precise target of the resistance, in early 2017, remained nebulous. Furthermore, we didn't want to launch an event founded on the negative: on rebuttal and condemnation. Instead, we wanted our literary protest to be visionary. To protect the American idea—democracy, pluralism, free expression—we had to present an American idea, from inception to present, worth fighting for.

To find that American idea, we organizers began combing through the rich archive of American protest literature.

From the start, American literature was driven by dual impulses: to preserve Western Enlightenment ideals and, simultaneously, to push away from conservative European tradition. These two impulses carried on together for over a century, well past the formation of the United States. Protest against political and religious authority was fundamental to American literature, and some of the most brilliant early American texts emerged from and helped shape the American instinct toward resistance. American writers ever since have sharpened their poetry, fiction, and polemic into weapons of political change.

We recruited thirty-five poets, novelists, journalists, translators, and essayists to read from legacy and contemporary texts that would resonate in the climate of resistance forming against the incoming president. With Trump taking aim at free expression and civil rights; immigrants, Muslims, gay, lesbian, and transgender people; environmental protection, research science, and inquiry; and even protest itself, Philadelphia Writers Resist beckoned to the voices of its literary ancestors and contemporaries to inspire the public into a mode of opposition. After all, American freedoms have been earned, one at a time, by people willing to articulate them and then fight to make them real.

As we began assembling the readings, we came to recognize the iterative, and often dialectic, nature of American protest writing: texts in various genres come together in a centuries-long conversation about the meaning of liberty. The religious visions of Puritan and Quaker writers, written in a spirit of imaginative dissent, established a framework for others like Thomas Paine, Thomas Jefferson, and James Madison to follow. And that was only the start. We chose several texts that turned the words of the Declaration of Independence and the U.S. Constitution against their authors, who directed the freedoms granted in those documents to white men only. In a 1799 petition, the Reverend Absalom Jones, a leader of the free black community of Philadelphia, mounted "We the People" with subversive force against the protectors of the slave trade. In 1876—which marked both the American centennial and the end of Reconstruction—Susan B. Anthony and members of the National Woman Suffrage Association aimed the Declaration of Independence back at its signers and, by corollary, America's image of itself, asserting that "the men of America are political monarchs, with their wives, their sisters, and their daughters as subjects."[2]

Times of unease, as we have learned, provoke reactionary political movements, as well as progressive ones, and our twentieth-century readings also emerged from particular moments of conflict and contention. The 1930s produced Langston Hughes's "Let America Be America Again"—a prescient rebuke to Trump's slogan, "Make America Great Again"—and President Franklin Roosevelt's 1936 Democratic Convention speech, which invoked the Declaration of Independence to oppose economic tyranny. The movements against racial injustice, pollution, and war in the 1960s engendered an extraordinary range of American protest writing; we chose passages from James Baldwin, Allen Ginsberg, and Martin Luther King Jr. The economic crisis of 2008 and the election of the first African American president, Barack Obama, and the backlash it produced, marked another period of literary resistance. During the Obama administration, literary protest helped define struggles for women's and gay rights and for multiculturalism. From this deep pool of poetry, prose, and polemic, we chose readings from Grace Lee Boggs, Gloria Anzaldua, Shirley Geok-Lin Lim, Naomi Shihab Nye, and Claudia Rankine.

On January 15, we rallied, and on January 20, 2017, Donald J. Trump was sworn in as the forty-fifth president of the United States. While Trump's early term has been bogged down by infighting and incompetence, he has indeed followed through on the promises—implicit and explicit—of his campaign. He has elevated white supremacists to high positions in the Oval Office and organized a cabinet largely of white male conservative evangelical Christians; attempted to institute religion-based travel bans, increased immigration raids and deportations, and discontinued Deferred Action for Childhood Arrivals (DACA), the program that protects the children of undocumented immigrants from deportation; dismantled government safety and environmental protections; and instigated international conflict. He continually threatens journalists, whom he has called "the enemy of the American people."[3] The only voices that seem to matter speak for wealth, whiteness, and privilege.

In 1976, Barbara Jordan followed her question "Who will speak for America?" with "Who then will speak for the common good?"[4] She indeed equated the idea of America with the notion of the common good, based on inclusion, equality, and generosity. These ideals, in sharp contrast to those of the president and his party, form a thread of this book. The question of who will speak for America is perhaps the most urgent of our time, as it begs us, as a nation, to look in the mirror—and at each other.

The contributors to this anthology—among them immigrants and refugees, men and women of color, gay and trans people, Christians, Jews, and Muslims—tackle the question of American identity and society, offering visions rooted in our history but attentive to our future. In *Who Will Speak for America?* we offer these visions: of pain, of fear, of resilience, of love, of confusion, of terror, of bravado, of absurdity, of beauty, of dystopia and utopia, of history, and of the future. The contributors continue the conversation that the American colonists began and that generations of activists, in their efforts to perfect our union, have elevated and amplified.

In Part I, "Speaking to America," writers address their attention to their families in the first days after the election (in the section "To Our Families"), to their own mental and emotional landscape during the first months of the administration (section "To Ourselves"), and to the country, already beset by racial injustice, poverty, misogyny, and violence (section "To Our Americas"). In Part II, "Speaking for America," writers wrestle with the meaning of America and American identity and imagine diverse futures (section "For the Nation"). Some of these futures necessitate practical political change, patience, organizing, and resilience; others depend on the elemental power of community (section "For the Future").

. . .

The Obama years brought encouraging signs of social progress: a steep reduction in the uninsured, legal gains for gay and transgender people, a drop in the federal incarceration rate, and a vast increase in accepted refugees. The America of 2016 was becoming more inclusive and more tolerant *for the common good*. The culmination of this might have been the inauguration of a new kind of president—the first woman president—as poet Eileen Myles, who ran for president in 1992, imagines in "Acceptance Speech (Nov 6 2016)," the preamble to this book. Myles unfurls a national plan for fairness, love, compassion, and fun. "We're going to massively fund libraries," Myles writes, "open twenty-four hours, and they will not be filled with homeless people because they will have homes, so the libraries will be filled with people reading and watching movies, and going into the conversation rooms and having conversations and so on." Myles reminds us that on November 8, 2016, we lost not only the progress intrinsic in electing the first female president but also the privilege of dreaming beyond the borders of banal political discourse. As we learned during the Writers Resist protest in Philadelphia, we must not condemn but imagine anew; as Myles instructs, we must open the library of American voices to everyone.

Yet, here in the present, the election and the first year of the Trump administration have shattered any sense of American well-being. "Today America screams, *'Go back to where you came from!'* which I take to mean / back to the darkness inside her," writes Joy Ladin in "America in Winter," the clear-eyed poem that sets the scene for Part I. Trump's reactionary policies may turn out to be a temporary reversal—the march to freedom is long and the road often rutted—but nevertheless, the president bears down on us, breaking up immigrant families; sending other immigrants into hiding; deputizing sexual predators and white supremacists, neo-Nazis and nativists; and eviscerating the government regulatory structures that protect us from environmental and safety risks. The effect has disturbed the most intimate form of our communal lives: the family.

In "To Our Families," a haunting essay by Carmen Maria Machado and a defiant poem by KC Trommer situate the injury of the election within the realm of private family memory. Other writers, like the scholar Tahneer

Oksman, the novelist Diane McKinney-Whetstone, and the poet Adam Vines, observe themselves and their children processing the fear and confusion of reactionary political change. Parent-child conversations in the weeks and months after the election are both fraught and a kind of solace; Melissa Febos extends the conversation to her students, whom she wants to protect as much as enlighten and inspire. The inauguration, writes Herman Beavers in the poem "20 January 2017," is "time to consider the whereabouts / of the precious and the prized." As the fiction writer Sarah Rose Etter seeks perhaps the impossible—to reconcile her political beliefs with her father's pro-Trump opinions—Bassey Ikpi carefully observes the relationship between her ten-year-old son and her elderly father in the months after the election. She concludes, "This is where my hope lives."

In our invitation to these writers, we asked them to consider "American ideals, identity, and citizenship in this age of political crisis and opportunity" and suggested that they might evoke or educate, provoke or reflect, or explore an explicitly personal dimension. So often, as in Ikpi's narrative, political changes refract inside the space of our personal lives. Literary writers, perhaps more than journalists or historians, have the capacity, or freedom, to shift scales, from the intimate and communal to the personal and interior and back out again to our wider society.

As we reconsider our relationship to our country as citizens and families, we must grapple with our own beliefs and psychological experience as unpredictable, terrifying, and destabilizing events unfold. In "To Ourselves," science fiction and fantasy writer Fran Wilde confronts Trump and GOP leaders' deception and doublespeak on plans for health care, taxes, and the environment: "That morning the officials / stole all the words" and turned them "upside down." Similarly, the cartoonist Liana Finck portrays her attempt to assimilate the political chaos, fear, and confusion of 2017. Finck observes life under Trump, a serial liar and abuser, whose power comes from displaying constant shifts in belief, or "gaslighting." The effect of gaslighting on the abused may be, as she suggests, emotional distance and denial. Juan Martinez embodies this feeling in the figure of the abyss:

The abyss asks that you please not laugh.
His retinue says the same. The retinue

of little abysses demands respect, silence,
a smidgen of fear. Won't you please fear him,

please? Won't you shake at the immensity
of his nothingness? Won't you cry or rage

or at the very least call back? We're lonely
here with the abyss, say the little abysses.

The dissonance has been exacerbated by the intrusion of the Trump regime into our personal lives—conversations are hijacked, leisure time replaced by organizing and protesting, and sleep interrupted. In the poem "Reclaiming Time," Airea D. Matthews describes a sleepless night filled with worry: "When the sun rises," she asks, "will the sickness value / your sons above a sweat bead, field, or ring?"

Novelist Ken Kalfus also tackles our new experience of time. He expresses a desire to "seize a moment" to slow the "blur of news" and writes against the abyss by documenting three random days of the Trump era, "if only so that I will understand how these days were actually experienced before they became a segment in the arc of a longer history, given new meaning by future events." That longer arc of history is the subject of an essay by the novelist Madeleine Thien, introducing her English translation of excerpts from the Cambodian writer Khun Srun's work *The Accused*. The translation reveals, in harrowing melancholy, the experience of a man living under tyranny and terror. Thien wants us to meditate on this particular "storm of history," asking how a person can "live a moral life in a time of devastating, and escalating, violence."

"These walls surrounding me are their laws, their police, their prisons, their guns," writes Khun, who was executed by the Khmer Rouge in 1978.

Walls are their business, trade, and profit.
All that subjugates people.
All that reduces them to the rank of objects.

"I fear the world we are unleashing," writes Thien, who argues for a radical awareness of the Other that could lead to nonviolence.

But is political violence ever justifiable? The novelist Sandra Newman shares four beguiling short histories that force us to question our values and instincts. Fiction writer Sam Miller, in the story "Yellow for Ephemeral," considers the search for purpose amid tragedy. Along with Newman and Thien, Miller asks us not only to observe and face the abyss but to dwell in it, for in confusion there is always hope for clarity.

In confronting the abyss, we acknowledge that it has always been here; we must investigate and document the society that created Trump. We need to frame and reframe, approach and reapproach until we understand the forces that produced this political crisis—or at the very least know what kinds of questions to ask. In this way, the novelists, essayists, and poets in "To Our Americas" face the nation that brought us to the 2016 election. They ask

America to lay its violence bare, without necessarily needing an answer or expecting a response.

In an excerpt from his novel *Year of the Rat*, Marc Anthony Richardson explores how incarceration poisons African American men. Poet Jericho Brown excoriates the terrorizing and murder of black men by police officers in "Bullet Points" and further explores the particularly American objectification and commodification of bodies in "The Legend of *Big* and *Fine*":

> Long ago, we used two words
> For the worth of a house, a car,
> A woman—all the same to men
> Who claimed them: things
> To be entered, each to suffer
> Wear and tear with time

These themes of fear, violation, and possession carry through the poems of Cynthia Atkins and Lynn Melnick. In "Domestic Terrorism," Atkins evokes the fear the powerful (men and boys, bosses) use against the powerless (prisoners, girls, employees). "I'll tell you about terror, the kind you feel when the neighborhood boys are chasing you home to see what's under your skirt, the downy fur between your legs. They want to own it," she writes.

In "National Pastime," Melnick meditates on the portrayal of rape. "Anything can be begged into art," she writes, warning us that our attempts to make sense of America's sickness might merely further our own obsessive desire for creation. In "Who Has the Right to Tell This Story?" the novelist Liz Moore asks a similar question: What is the role of the artist in portraying the suffering of others? Along with the photographer Jeffrey Stockbridge, she revisits recovering addicts, many of them sex workers, she interviewed years ago in Kensington, a Philadelphia neighborhood devastated by the opioid epidemic. She speaks to therapists and community activists in an effort to understand the possibility and limits of art to reshape narratives and reform lives.

Indeed, we as writers want to know: What are we accomplishing? Perhaps we're giving dimension to suffering and also renewal. These things can't be real to you, the reader, or to us, as writers, unless we write them. Through literature we become responsible for each other, for the present and the future. "I am on a cross where time and space intersect," writes Alice Notley, the poet, in "I Enter the Real Memory."

> You come and go via me   the crystal exaltation
> And the keeper of the layers of speaking and knowing:
> You are in my hands.

Perhaps the point of asking a rhetorical question like "Who will speak for America?" is to assert that we all—including the incarcerated and murdered, the abused and neglected among us—speak for the nation. And in speaking for it, we keep each other in our hands, as a society of linked interests, each person treating the other fairly—a radical view in Trump's America. Because, as Edwin Torres writes in his poem "Who Will Speak for Whom, America?" in Part II:

> most of humanity is used to showing emotion, used to showing
> compassion, empathy, honor, humility, human traits that characterize us
> as human beings who understand another's plight, another's approach

Torres helps us make the turn from speaking to America to speaking for it, arguing that as individuals and a collective "we," we ought not lose ourselves in the speaking. Otherwise we each might lose the very humanity that makes our speech matter. We live in an age of verbal excess—politicians' deceit and doublespeak, a frenzied media landscape, and a digital environment that allows marginalized voices to thrive while also giving new power to propagandists and hate speech. Words are simultaneously more and less powerful.

How can our voices overcome the powerful segmentation of American society? Do we speak for our own identity group, for those without voice, for all humans, for some construct of "America"? Do we speak for us, today, or for the future? Do we somehow speak to the past that seems to inspire and taunt, that never relents? Do we reaffirm a historical sense of Americanness? If so, on what basis?

In asking these questions we might return to Barbara Jordan and her 1976 speech to the Democratic National Convention:

> I could list the problems which cause people to feel cynical, angry, frustrated: problems which include lack of integrity in government; the feeling that the individual no longer counts; the reality of material and spiritual poverty; the feeling that the grand American experiment is failing or has failed. I could recite these problems, and then I could sit down and offer no solutions. But I don't choose to do that either. The citizens of America expect more. They deserve and they want more than a recital of problems.
>
> We are a people in a quandary about the present. We are a people in search of our future. We are a people in search of a national community. We are a people trying not only to solve the problems of the present, unemployment, inflation, but we are attempting on a larger

scale to fulfill the promise of America. We are attempting to fulfill our national purpose, to create and sustain a society in which all of us are equal.[5]

The writers in this book answer Jordan's call. The act of being American, they show, is an act of personal and civic imagination and experimentation, of conjuring what America is and what it could be. Just as those who have claimed various rights and responsibilities have always done, speaking for America means interrogating its complexities while protecting its singular ideas of liberty, justice, and equality.

In "For the Nation," poet Cynthia Arrieu-King describes the ongoing making of her American identity as she negotiates her place within her communities. Samira Ahmed also portrays her Americanness as a process. She learns rejection as a child, learns the rules for acceptance as a young woman, and ultimately reclaims her American identity by asserting her whole self: "You claim your joy. / You lay your roots: / Blood and bone and fire and ash. / And in this land of the free and home of the brave, you plant yourself. / Like a flag."

Novelist Carlos José Pérez Sámano, a recent immigrant, wonders if America will force him to mask his Mexican-formed self or if it will embrace that self. He envisions an American culture built of the "little differences" of immigrants from all over the world, one that acknowledges its connection to the thirty-six countries that make up the continents that share its name. In "Blood and Spirit," poet Cynthia Dewi Oka explores the emotional landscape of a refugee about to cross the border to the United States, to "enter America (future / tense)."

In both poetry and prose, Mohja Kahf also recognizes the little differences that we share as children, as activists, and as minorities, along with our indelible global connections. She imagines an America, and a world, that makes room for the self and Americans who learn from each other's experience of—and fights against—oppression.

In speaking for America, we must face up to the absurdity of a brash, militaristic, and hungry America that devours and commodifies our differences. This is Herman Beavers's reminder in "Untitled: A Comedy." Writer Linh Dinh, in "Pigskin, Beauty, Death, and a Huggable Rat," and poet Craig Santos Perez, in "America (after Allen Ginsberg)," stretch Beavers's comedy to expose the sickness of an insatiable nation. "Much more than land, America invades minds," Dinh writes. "There is scarcely a brain alive that's not / Constantly titillated and harassed by / American culture."

How can any of us speak for this domineering nation that calls itself "America," as if to claim half the world? The poet and fiction writer Ana-

Maurine Lara seconds Pérez Sámano's call to imagine America, the nation, embedded in its hemisphere, of a piece with North and South and Central America, while at the same time the product of its unique polyglot history, the sum total of little differences. Seeing America this way, as "América," her body stretching "from the silver sun of the Arctic / to the blazing blue of Antarctica," transforms our vision and with it our sense of what's possible. When Lara writes, in the refrain of her poem "América," "I do not speak for América; / I cannot contain América," it isn't because she lacks a voice but because América—America—is an immeasurable thing.

This immeasurability demands radical imagination; our future demands the same. We begin the final section of the book, "For the Future," with a drawing by the fiction writer and cartoonist Adrienne Celt. Here is the body of America, the dry desert mesa of Arizona, where Celt lives, and the faces of black, brown, and white women on horseback, uniting in a stampede. This is "Life After," a vision of the America that was already forming before Trump—egalitarian, determined, and well aware of the long road ahead. Rene Denfeld, novelist and death-penalty investigator who works to exonerate the innocent and find mercy for the guilty, describes this long road in her essay "The Gates to Freedom." She writes:

> Right now, many of us feel like my clients, trapped in terrifying circumstances that are out of our control. And like my clients, we are hoping someone will show up with a key and release us. But that is not going to happen. It's going to take us a long time to remedy the political crisis and to reverse injustice and inequality, just as it took us a long time to get here.

Denfeld's essay is sobering but also hopeful. She traces Trump's victory, in part, to mass incarceration—of African Americans, who have been disenfranchised, and whites, who have been radicalized in prison as neo-Nazis and white nationalists. Her success relies on careful and relentless work, a model for all of us who fight for a more just society. The nonfiction writer Veronica Scott Esposito provides another model for achieving a just future: the recent history of California, whose electorate has transformed from politically reactionary and anti-immigrant in the 1990s to progressive today. Esposito's essay, "If You Can Keep It," draws not only on California's recent history but on her own, as a once-happy young conservative who cheered anti-immigrant measures. She locates her personal change in her study of early American political history and the Constitution's Enlightenment ideals. To fight cyclical waves of illiberalism—like the one we face today—we must bolster education about our founding principles and, foremost, "be courageous. Be ambitious."

And if our courage and ambition fail? Ganzeer, an exiled Egypt-born artist and writer who now lives in Denver, describes a futuristic earth colonized by waves of interplanetary immigrants, replicating the tension between Americans' ideals and Americans' worst tendencies. His story, "Charlie and the Aliens," does not shy away with from the damage of our society's approach to immigration, but it retains a hopeful note: that American core values of liberty, equality, and justice are unkillable. In "The End of the Incarnation," Malka Older, a specialist and scholar in international aid and development, envisions a mass secession from the United States. As borders shift and disappear, the country's disintegration culminates in the flourishing of a new ideal: one's birthplace should have no bearing on one's rights.

Novelist and editor Charlie Jane Anders ends the book with a depiction of communities forming, failing, and reforming after a far-future destruction of American civilization. "Because Change was the Ocean and We Lived by Her Mercy" ends with a vision of enduring—if imperfect and ever precarious—community. "Then we went back to staring down at the wasteland," says the narrator of Anders's story, "trying to imagine how many generations it would take before something green came out of it."

And so the work—and the questions, the arguments, the personal stories and fantasies and poems—continues. Just like the historical authors of our collected resistance texts, we find ourselves in another moment of political crisis. Writers, as well as musicians, performers, and visual artists, are being transformed by the moment; their work, some of it collected here, will come to define the resistance and the future shape and direction of American civic life. They are continuing the conversation the earliest American resistance writers began.

The answer to the question "Who will speak for America?," it may turn out, is the repetition of the question itself. As the central question of the American experiment, it begs us to ask and to listen.

Notes

1. Barbara Jordan, keynote address to the Democratic National Convention, July 12, 1976, New York, available at http://www.americanrhetoric.com/speeches/barbarajordan 1976dnc.html.

2. Dee Brown, *The Year of the Century: 1876* (New York: Scribner, 1966), 145.

3. Michael M. Grynbaum, "Trump Calls the News Media the 'Enemy of the American People,'" *New York Times*, February 17, 2017, available at https://www.nytimes.com/2017/02/17/business/trump-calls-the-news-media-the-enemy-of-the-people.html.

4. Jordan, keynote address.

5. Ibid.

PREAMBLE

ACCEPTANCE SPEECH
(NOV 6 2016)

Eileen Myles

First I want to say this feels incredible. To be female, to run and run and run to not see any end in sight but maybe have a feeling that there's really no outside to this endeavor this beautiful thing. You know we don't have a single female on any of our bills. And what about two women, two women loving. Or even more. A lot of women. A lot of money. Is there a message that I failed to receive that the face of woman cannot be on our money. And what about that house I just won. that white one. When I sit there and if I sit there and I've got to tell you I'm not sure I want to sit there. Some of you might remember my first campaign yes that was back in 1992. Few men have run for twenty-four years. Twenty-five by the time I stand and take the oath in January to serve my country. I did not quit I stand here with you on this beautiful rapturous day sunny day in New York to turn around, to look back and look at all that we've won. But I'm getting ahead of myself. Let's get back to that house. That white house. We often hear these words even as an explanation of what metonym means. Are you familiar with this term. yes I promise you a poetic presidency. The white house speaks is a metonym. Certainly that white house we speak of is not the whole government. Like Fred Moten says it is incomplete. But it has come to be a symbol of it. And I think two things. I think whiteness, I think of the whiteness of the house and I think of house-ness. It houses the government. Now that I have won it offers to house me now. I now officially make that white house a homeless shelter. It is a complete total disgrace that we have people without homes living on the streets of America. I have lived with them. Not for long periods of time but in the same way that I am the first president who knows what women feel because I am a woman, I am one, I have also eaten chicken with the homeless. I ate at the Bowery mission. Very rubbery, very chewy chicken. Those chicken were not happy when they lived and they are no happier being chewed on dead at the Bowery mission, and the chewers are not happy either, no. So here's the future good food at the white house for all the homeless in America. You know who the homeless are. They are military men and women. Who fought our pointless wars, who came home after each stupid greedy war we have waged and they got less. Is there a GI bill for veterans of Iraq and Afghanistan. I'm not sure but I don't think so. Can they buy a house. Who can buy a house. Under

Myles they have bought the white house. That is my gift. The white house will house the mentally ill, out patiented during the great president Reagan, meaning he threw them out of the house, the mentally ill, thrown out of the American house, and the alcoholics who do not have free and abundant and available treatment? 'Cause this country breaks our hearts. We will habit them too. We will occupy all government buildings and memorials housing and holding and loving the homeless and the sick and the starving. We'll do what the statue says. you know liberty. We will take buildings and we will build buildings and our culture our new America will begin to live. Our government needs to be in the business of living not dying, what else is a government for. The government will become more departmental and take you in, you and your wonderful needs. We'll start with the Department of Women. Obviously to say women matter and do matter so much and a lot we need a distinct place in the government to specifically focus on female concerns which is parity mainly, reforming congress so that if America is increasingly diverse in a multitude of ways our congress must represent those groups percentage-wise that's smart don't you think. So if most of the people in America are female so should be our government right. America is not a department store. We want to do more in our country than shop online and at the mall. Let's face it everyone is home shopping and yelling at each other at their computers. The malls are falling apart. The malls are pretty much gone. Let them go. We want to make real departments for who we really are. Not shopping. We will be stalwart, we will be strong. Let's go. Let's go out. we are out there now. We are here on the highline. Yes.

That's the way it works under Myles. Early on I described a department of culture. We will have that. We will have art in America, not just the magazine, just for starters we will multiply the budget of the NEA by tenfold. We will bring back CETA, that was like an art workers program we had in the eighties but we will call it SEE THE . . . SEE THE . . . what I don't know. I just got elected, I haven't worked everything out but just think of the possibilities. SEE THE sky, SEE THE river over there, SEE THE Whitney, a lot of people will be walking around appreciating and we will pay them. There will also be the HEAR THE program, the SMELL THE program. That's probably what you're going to do early on with all those you know recovering veterans who don't have to live on the streets. Get them in on the SEE THE, SMELL THE, HEAR THE programs. We're going to massively fund libraries, open twenty-four hours, and they will not be filled with homeless people because they will have homes, so the libraries will be filled with people reading and watching movies, and going into the conversation rooms and having conversations and so on. All education will be free, trains will be free. Cars will eventually be banned.

Cars are stupid. No more pumping oil, no more fracking. Everything will be driven by the sun, or else be plugged in electrically. Electric something. There'll be lots of free food. A lot of archery. Everyone will be a really good shot. We'll get good at aiming, intentions, not killing. Oh yeah and we'll send a lot of masseuses to Israel and Palestine. Everyone needs a good rub. No more pesticides, here, anywhere, lots of small farmers, an amazing number of stand-up comedians, and lots of rehearsal spaces and available musical instruments and learning centers for people like myself who would like to play something, perhaps a guitar. Nobody would be unemployed. Everyone would be learning Spanish, or going to the sex center for a while having ejaculation contests, or just looking at porn for a while and going out into the yard and helping the farmers improve the crops. Just gardening. Helping the flowers. Distributing the flowers. SEE THE flowers. When in doubt always just being a SEE THE person for a while. There'll be a whole lot of people encouraging people to SEE THE. We want the SEE THE to thoroughly come back. There'd be an increase in public computers, like water, like air, have we stopped the oil and the fracking early enough to protect the water and air, we hope so but there will be a decrease in private computers with an enhanced desire to be here, exactly here where we are, which some would argue is *there* on the computer which of course would be allowed but being *here* would be cool, some people meditating, other people just walking around, smiling feeling good about themselves, living shamelessly and glad. Guns would be buried. Guns would be in museums and people would increasingly not want to go there. Gun museums would die. What was that all about. Money would become rare. I would have a radio show as your president and also I might be on television and also I just might want to talk to you. In the tradition of American Presidents like Fiorello La Guardia the little Flower I would be president Edward Myles, the woman, changing my name, very often, would probably be good I would like that and I would write a new poem for you each week. I might just walk around saying it and eventually you would forget I was the president. I would go to the gym. There are people who like to manage things just like there are people who like to play cards and the managers would change often enough and they would keep the parks clean, America increasingly turning into one big park, one big festival of existence with unmarked toilets and nightly daily events and free surfing lessons and free boards, just put it back when you're done and a good bed for everyone, I just slept in the best bed last night and I slept on the plane sleep is great nobody would be short of sleep everyone would be well slept, chaotic and loving hearted and have all the time in the world to not kill, to love and be president everyone take your turn and dance. Dance now. I love my fellow citizens. It is good to win. Thank you. I feel like I had a bad dream last night that like the head of the FBI decided to steal the election by making shit up about me because I am female but that wasn't true and we are really here undeluded, un mucked up. Wide awake in America for once. SEE THE SEE THE SEE all of your fabulous beauty and your power and your hope. Thanks for your vote. And I love you so much thanks.

PART I

SPEAKING TO AMERICA

AMERICA IN WINTER

Joy Ladin

Snow on the train tracks, snow on the haunches
of stump-starred slopes, extractor frozen into Sunday silence.

Daylight in heaven, evening on earth,
America stumbling between them.

America's lost; we all know that.
America's been served one too many

lattes, eviction notices, summonses.
I fell for America in high school.

Every now and then, I tell myself she's catching my eye,
dreaming, like me, of growing old together

if we both survive. She's the only country I've ever wanted, the only one
who could finish my sentences.

God, she's beautiful without her clothes.
When we were fifty years younger, we walked on the moon together.

Today America screams, *"Go back to where you came from!"* which I take to
    mean
back to the darkness inside her.

Rumor has it she can't remember what she means.
Amnesia gives her an air of innocence,

but America has thieved and lied, fattened herself
on slavery and genocide

and has a long, troubled history
of blowing holes in folks who try to save her.

Now America's brushing her clouds
with gold she hasn't stolen,

promising to hold me the way she holds
her mountains and her rivers.

I tell her I'm bitter. How can we go on, I ask her,
if we've become monsters to one another?

For the first time in my life,
we're alone together. Then I realize

the night is starred
left and right, far and wide

with hearts as broken
as America's and mine.

To Our Families

HOW I SHOULD HAVE KNOWN TRUMP WOULD BE ELECTED PRESIDENT

Carmen Maria Machado

Because a few days before the election, I was walking in a garden and saw a pulse of motion and realized there was a hawk in the grass a few feet away from me, and when he turned his cruel and terrible head, I saw a dead mouse hanging heavily in his beak like a testicle.

Because that hawk looked right at me before he took off flying, and from the branch where he landed, there was a *rip, rip*, and entrails unraveled like yarn.

Because once, my uncle showed me all of his guns, and there were so many of them lined up in a drawer beneath his bed, and the ammunition rattled in its box like movie theater candy.

Because in October, it snowed, and even though I love snow, I took no pleasure in it.

Because when I was a girl we visited a North Carolina beach town with my family, and my father went out one afternoon to get us groceries and came back in a strange mood, and it was over a year later when he confessed to my mother that he did not wish to return to the North Carolina coast for vacation because locals had yelled unrepeatable racial slurs at him when he came out of the store with hamburgers and buns.

Because I made a wedding scrapbook, and the first page was just pictures of lesbian brides cut out of magazines, and every time I looked at it, I felt happy and sappy and sentimental.

Because a few years back I was sitting in a quiet car with my mother and two of her sisters, and one of them said, "I just don't believe in gay people," and I laughed, startled, because it sounded like she meant gay people didn't exist, like unicorns, and so I said to her, "Well, we believe in you, Auntie," and the car was silent again.

Because when my conservative, devoutly Catholic grandmother died, I was grateful she was dead and that I never had to come out to her.

Because on Election Day I went grocery shopping and parked next to a massive pickup truck with a Trump bumper sticker, and when I walked past it, I found myself giving it wide berth, like it was radiating heat.

Because when I was growing up, we lived next to an older white gay couple who told my parents that they hoped me and my siblings would get run over by a car and that our "type of people" didn't belong on that side of Allentown, and so my father had my mother give him a haircut on the front porch, where he sat shirtless drinking red wine and blasting salsa music at full volume.

Because not too soon after that, I took a tomato from the couple's garden, and my mother marched me over to their house to apologize and return the stolen fruit, and I proffered it to them like it was a human heart, and the thin skin was broken, and it was leaking acidic juice that ran down my skinny arms, and they looked uncomfortable and said it was fine, I could keep the tomato, and then as we were leaving, I asked them if they were married to each other, and my mother hustled me outside before they could answer.

Because on Sunday, that last Sunday, the clocks went back an hour, and instead of noticing the earlier sunrise, I noticed only the earlier darkness.

NOTE

This essay was previously published as Carmen Maria Machado, "How I Should Have Known Trump Would Be Elected President," *HTMLGiant*, November 10, 2016, available at http://htmlgiant.com/random/how-i-should-have-known-trump-would-be-elected-president.

TEACHING AFTER TRUMP

Melissa Febos

The day before the 2016 presidential election, I taught a literature class to twenty-five students, few of them English majors. I work in a red county in New Jersey, at a private university where Trump was elected by a small margin in our undergraduate student body's straw poll. Our student population is more than 60 percent white, with a high number of first-generation college students. Despite it being an hour's drive away, many of them have never been to Manhattan. Most of them have never left the country, and some not even the county—for lack of motivation rather than resources. I often struggle to relate to them academically; I was an intellectually ambitious, highly politicized college student who idealized radical feminist thinkers and was so motivated to learn that I wrote a senior thesis twice as long as was expected.

I suspect that my students are a pretty ordinary sample of their generation. They are also, on the whole, kind, good-natured, and teachable. Some are incredibly talented and perceptive. In my four years of teaching them, I have calibrated my curriculum to reach them where they are, and a lot of the time it does. This requires a kind of pedagogic creativity that isn't taught in graduate school, and reaching them is rewarding in ways that I couldn't have anticipated.

I teach them about feminism without ever uttering the word *feminism*, because I know how instantly the word will alienate my students. I teach intersectionality without ever defining it. I fill my syllabi with women and writers of color and don't announce it. My students don't seem to notice. But they read the books. And when I see that flicker of awakening in their faces as they discuss James Baldwin or Jesmyn Ward or Junot Diaz or Joy Harjo and connect their own sympathies with people different from them, sometimes for the first time, I am grateful that I teach here and not at a school where the undergraduates are already fluent in the jargon of hegemony, diaspora, paradigm, and intersectionality.

I had planned a discussion of *Narrative of the Life of Frederick Douglass, an American Slave*. As usual, we opened class with a couple of student presentations on the text. There were five obvious students of color in the literature class, three of them young black women. One of these gave the first presentation. A quieter student, she passed out her handout and stood at the front of the classroom. In a trembling voice, she faced the room full of her white classmates and began to explain race as a social construction. She stumbled and searched for her words. She clenched the piece of paper in her hand, with its bulleted notes. The topic of her presentation was the "ethical content" of the assigned text, and in this halting manner, but with her head held high, she discussed the "ethics" of slavery. Just after she described the way slave women had their newborn infants taken from them and sold to other plantations, she paused and stared out at the silent class. She blinked. "Just imagine," she said. And then continued.

I don't think the other students saw the tears in my eyes as she spoke, but they heard me clap for a long time after she finished. I wanted to carry her out of that classroom on my shoulders. But I knew there was no place to carry her. As I clapped, I offered a silent, fervent prayer that this election's result would be a step toward a world in which she was safe.

. . .

Since childhood, my grief has had a prayerful refrain, for safety: *I want to go home.*

I grew up in a loving home. My mother was, and still is, a Buddhist psychotherapist and staunch feminist. My father is a Puerto Rican sea captain. They are both Democrats and are both from working-class towns in New Jersey much like the one where I teach. I spent my early life carrying signs in peaceful marches and reading while my mother attended meetings of our local National Organization for Women chapter. I also spent a lot of my childhood waiting for my father to return from sea.

"I want to go home," I whispered alone in my bedroom at eight years old, missing him. "I want to go home," I whispered alone in my bedroom at twelve years old after fighting with a class of fellow sixth graders about my right to love another woman. "I want to go home," I whispered alone in my bedroom at fourteen after a senior boy grabbed my breast in the high school hallway, meeting my eyes defiantly as he stared down at me. "I want to go home," I whispered alone in my bedroom at twenty after shooting speedballs, terrified of the day that my family would find out by way of my dead body. "I want to go home," I whispered alone in my bedroom at thirty-six years old on the morning that Donald Trump became our president-elect.

The home that I longed for at eight years old, at twelve and fourteen and twenty and thirty-six, was not a literal place. It was a feeling. It was a faith that I, and the people I loved, would be safe. That whatever pain we suffered would pass without killing us, or the parts of us we needed to survive, to thrive, to create love and art and social change.

No matter what our age, this kind of despair manifests in the same way: as a wish that someone will rescue us. A parent, God, a place inside ourselves where we can find refuge and reassurance that everything will be okay.

. . .

How could I face my students the day after the election? Ten years ago, when I began teaching, I trained myself to hide my politics. For the first five years, I even hid my tattoos. Not out of shame but out of protection. And because I wanted to do my job effectively. I wanted to teach students who had different beliefs than me to love literature, to believe in the inherent value and power of art. To understand how much of our history is archived there. I wanted to turn them into bibliophiles, champions of human rights, believers in their power as compassionate citizens. And most of the time I knew my best chance of succeeding meant hiding how desperately I wanted to succeed.

But Professor Febos did not feel like someone I could be that day. I could only be this devastated woman who wanted to go *home*. This queer woman sunk in terror for her country. For her loved ones. For all black and brown and immigrant and queer and trans and disabled and female people. For all the boy children, white children, and girls in her country who would learn how to be men, or white, or women—how to be Americans under Donald Trump's administration.

And then, like so many times before, I remembered the person who had always rescued me. The person within me who had built her entire life around the ways she could best keep herself and her loved ones and her country safe. The person who had become a teacher and a writer for precisely those reasons. Because in a country whose government we do not trust, who do we need more than writers and teachers? And what is more powerful than an inspired youth? I turned off the radio. The newscasters would not make it okay. My parents would not make it okay. My students were our best hope. And I could reach them faster than anyone.

I walked into the classroom where I teach my Introduction to Creative Writing seminar and told my fifteen students to take out their notebooks. I had no idea what I was going to say to them. My heart pounded as I stared at their expectant faces. Out of the fifteen, twelve were young white women and the other two were young men of color. I had no idea their politics, though I would wager at least a couple of them voted for Trump. I had no desire to alienate any of them. As they dug into their backpacks and produced their pens, I stared at them. I scoured my insides for some trust that underneath whatever differences, we all harbored an earnest desire for the safety and freedom of other humans. To my relief, I found it, a warm ember in my gut that seemed to glow when I touched it.

I told my students to describe a person opposite them in the most obvious ways: race, religion, sexual orientation, and country of origin. When their pens slowed, I asked them to describe the country they wish for that person. After a few more minutes, I asked them to think of a child they loved—their own, a niece or nephew, an infant version of themselves. I asked them to describe the country in which they wished that child to come of age.

I watched them as they wrote—their smooth foreheads crimped with concentration, their hands moving across notebook pages. When they looked up, I asked them to reconcile those visions into a single vision of a country where both of those realities could exist and both people would be free to inhabit them. They stared at me for a few beats and then began writing. Some of them paused, pens hovering over paper as they stared into space and worked out some detail in their minds. They wrote for a long time. When the scratching of pens quieted, I took a deep breath. Something had shifted in the room. We all felt it. As if there was an ember in each of them, stoked by their pens, that had glowed warm and bright enough for us all to see.

"I want," I said, searching for my next move. "I want you to make a list." They laughed, first quietly and then louder, because this was how I started so many of their in-class exercises and because they needed so badly to laugh. "I want you to make a list of all the things you can do to build this home for us." This time, many of them nodded. They understood what I was asking them to do.

The room changed that day, the way it does when the space between who my students are in public and who they are inside themselves closes a little. When they take a risk and reveal something that scares them. But that day, I revealed something, too. I try to keep my own needs out of my classroom. They need me to hold the space, and it's harder for me to do that if I hold a personal stake. But I suspect that my students understood that I needed them to collaborate with me, to imagine something better than what the morning had promised us. And they had. My students had written about their immigrant grandparents, the people they most loved, the unspoken and spoken divisions in their homes and communities. Even those students whom I suspected voted for Trump were careful in their exercises, generous in their vision. It's hard not to be when faced with the earnest fears of people you know. At the end of that class, I offered an open invitation for anyone to come talk to me about the election and any reaction they might have. They came. Many said it was the first time they'd spoken aloud about their fears, the ways they silently disagreed with their families. They stumbled to name their ambivalence, the disappointment they felt after voting in their first election. "It's bad, isn't it?" a few of them asked in the quiet of my office. "Yes," I said. And later that semester, after Trump's travel ban, they came back again. "It's bad, isn't it?" they asked, sometimes tentatively, as if they might get in trouble for wondering. "Yes," I said. I'd never been so forthright about my own political opinions with students at this school.

In the months that have followed, my fear has settled from the searing terror and despair of that day into something quieter but no less persistent. Inside my office, I have continued being honest with them. Their political awareness is so new—if they cannot remember a time before the Trump era, it might easily become normal without the contrast of the Obama years. And of course, in the larger scope of history, it *is* normal. That has always been a part of my curriculum, though it has become a part of our conversations now, too.

They have not put away their lists. One of my students came to me and told me that she had started a hard conversation with her family. It went okay. Another told me that he came out to his. It didn't go as he'd hoped, but he isn't sorry he did it. I am not much of an idealist. I do not believe that my students are going to turn their families. That we will survive this administration without millions of casualties. That we will survive as a species who has so abused our resources. But I have been heartened to see that so many of my students envision honesty as part of our solution. That they have recognized the integrity of revealing themselves, even when they know others will disagree with what they think or even who they are. They have not long been forming beliefs independent from those they have inherited. It is a delicate and sometimes dangerous thing to think for yourself. Visibility is a powerful political tool. My hope is that this small knowledge, that there is enough room for everyone in a single classroom, is a belief that they can carry into the world. It will, soon enough, be theirs.

IUD

Liana Finck

20 JANUARY 2017

Herman Beavers

This morning, I delighted
to discover my heart thudding
in the same place in my chest.

Wiggled all my fingers and toes,
felt clothed in my right
mind. Then I re-

collected today is fraught
with calamity, sadness,
to the point that the sunlight

falls fractured, impure, corrupted.
Feel the weight of those frozen
in an amber of despair, im-

mobilized to tears or rage or tumult.
Hands wringing, the eye grows
anxious for a welcome place

to land; body and soul
seem ready to come unglued.
Time, I think, to ponder

the whereabouts. The
whereabouts of people you love
or want to love. The where-

abouts of the next great, good thing;
delight in the coming forth, the crouch
of insurrection's rampant audacity.

Time to consider the whereabouts
of the precious and the prized, the where-
abouts of the nomadic seeker

setting out once more. The destiny
of evanescent hopes, songs that
bind our hurts and make

the fractured whole. Time
to ascertain the grace abounding
from those who ponder *our whereabouts*;

the ecstasy of *there*.

SIGNS

Diane McKinney-Whetstone

I was glad for the signs
and for the women waving the signs
Especially after the despairing statistic that white women had broken
for Trump
Such an apt word, broken, to be in a state of disrepair
But there they were
a million or more unbroken in pink knitted pussy hats
And there I was
Black woman me feeling a hopeful vibe
despite the toxic sludge creeping, its too-long red tie trailing
into 1600

I pondered a particular sign
No images on that sign
of women flexing muscles
or wearing hijabs made of the American flag
Just the words *I'm too old to still be marching for the same shit*

A woman of a certain age myself, I thought it funny
I tried to laugh but could not
Mouth on fire from the searing truth
I tasted ash
This was some new shit, too

A confluence
Such a gentle word, *confluence,*
that should be describing lovely streams
meeting other streams in tender folds
frothily catching the light
making rainbows

But this confluence
was the dredging up of
some throwback hate
colluding with contemporaneous hate

composite hate
solid and liquefied hate
making sludge

I've known sludge
Get back, Black
you don't belong here
your life,
surely your son's life, does not matter sludge
Woman can't can't no, you certainly cannot sludge

But this sludge, with its stolen power
its calculated buffoonery
its bombastic rhetoric
unleashing the vile
while duping them
staining in full view
in hamlets and villages and Charlottesville
sans sheets or hoods
showcasing swastikas
widening the cracks
in a fragile progress
to bring the whole house down

This was some new shit

Though, as the sister's sign said,
it was the same old, same old, too
The stench of evil having leaked through the ages
from the entrails of tiny-handed men
battling for dominion over all things
Fixed on destroying what their contemptible selves yearn most to be
Loved

Like a river loved
flowing in thoughtful pleats
A gushing love
gyrating
Victorious hot springs love
like a geyser love burning away the hate
with eruptions from the center of the earth

that push up glorious displays of love thine own enemy
kind of love
Unfathomable to unascended me
But that's what the preacher said to do
and my grandmother, who was righteous
who rocked me to the same rhythm
that began time before there was even such hate
A perfect sway unbroken
growing never too old to march

MORNING QUESTION IN BED AFTER THE WOMEN'S MARCHES ACROSS AMERICA

Adam Vines

—For Mary

"Do we deserve to live?" you ask,
not do we live or how we live,
those I have stumbled through before,
dawn reticulating light through blinds
across the beds I built for your dolls.
Before I trip into an answer,
some softened Hume or backwoods Job,
or try to squeeze from you the doubt,
you blurt out Pilate's wife, the dream
she had, what you recall from Sunday's
service. You say that you woke up
last night from dreams of women dressed
in white all standing in the streets,
and as the light reveals your face,
a bar across your mouth and one
across your eyes, your words dissolve,
reform into a wrinkled sheet

of light I lift above my head to hear
and see beneath three million chant
in unison, "Our bodies are not yours."
You ask, "What is our only comfort in?"
I can't respond. I hide my face. "In us,"
you say for me with fortitude and grace.

FOUR DAYS

Sarah Rose Etter

I

The numbers come in. The party gets quiet. A woman stands up and leaves, slamming the door. The food, on the trays, goes untouched, hard, cold. The woman on the television keeps repeating that she doesn't believe it. In the corner, another woman turns her back to the room and begins to weep.

In the morning, the sky is gray. I step into the street as a woman I've never seen walks by. Our eyes meet, and we fall into each other's arms, weeping, warbling against each other.

At lunch, I poke a fork at my food. I live on the salt of broth, a silent protest. I imagine women across the city doing the same—mouths clenched, bodies tense, bones emerging from beneath skin.

For four days, my city is silent as a funeral, except for the protests, except for the helicopters, thundering overhead.

II

On the way to the protest, I hold posters beneath my arms. Women stream out of their work buildings in their professional clothes. They meet me on the corner. We walk down the street together, thirty or forty strong in the thin sunshine.

A man lifts his head as I pass.

"Guess who won?" he bellows. He flings his hand out, grabbing for my crotch.

A shot of terror rips through my body.

"Get your hands away from me!" I scream.

"Oh, you would have liked it," he says, spitting on the sidewalk.

Later, in the center of the city, I lift my sign high beneath the helicopters and scream until my throat splinters.

III

My father sits across from me, his stomach bulging, his flesh bigger than before. We are eating in my hometown: a suburb of small rolling green hills, power plant churning smoke, shuttered car dealerships, ribs of dogs lying exposed in alleys, drugged corpses of my high school friends.

"I'll have another," he says, pointing to his empty soda.

"Why did you do it?" I ask.

"Need to drain the swamp."

"A man tried to grab me in the street this week. He tried to grab me between the legs. There are protests every day."

"Nothing like that happening out here. We're all happy. You're overreacting. We spent eight years your way, and look where it got us."

The greased air of the restaurant clogs my nostrils. More french fries are delivered to the table.

"Another car dealership shut down, you know," my father says.

I picture the cars, shimmering in the sun and then crushed into piles of wrenched metal. I slide a french fry into my mouth. Through the window, beyond the green hills, the power plant churns up more perfect white smoke.

IV

My father drives to the city in a big, white car.

"Nice boat," I say and drop a kiss to his cheek.

We walk through my neighborhood in the sunlight, beneath the green trees. We find a restaurant with a table outside and order plates of eggs.

"You know what I hate about the city?" he asks.

"What?" I ask.

"Everything! The crowds, the traffic, it's all trash everywhere."

I picture his life at home: the same restaurant every Friday, the same television show every Saturday, the same salted pretzels for a snack, on the couch, in the living room. I picture the gate around the neighborhood of identical houses where I grew up.

"Aren't you worried about crime?" he asks. "Something bad is going to happen to you one of these days. I worry about you all the time."

I shake my head. I know the numbers. I know what's on the decline.

"It depends what kind of crime you mean," I say, picturing the face of the man who reached for my crotch, in the street, in broad daylight, in my city.

SEASONS OF GRIEF

Tahneer Oksman

That fall was my season of studying other people's grief.

In late 2016, I was working on a book about absence and mourning, reading all I could about what it means to lose someone close—a parent, a spouse, a child. How the experience can shatter your sense of self and place in the world. How grief can turn you into a stranger to yourself and others.

"I feel as if I'm missing something visible—an arm, a leg," writes Joyce Carol Oates in *A Widow's Story*, her record of the year or so after she suddenly lost her husband, the author and editor Raymond J. Smith. "Or that part of my face has been smudged and distorted as in a nightmare painting by Francis Bacon."[1]

The grieving, of course, are always among us, but it takes a special kind of sight to notice that they are there. In other words, you have to seek them out.

"People who have recently lost someone have a certain look," observes Joan Didion, another famous writer recording her husband's death in her now canonical *The Year of Magical Thinking*. "It is the look of someone who walks from the ophthalmologist's office into the bright daylight with dilated eyes, or of someone who wears glasses and is suddenly made to take them off."[2]

Recognizing the (almost) invisible pain of those walking among us can be a way of somehow sharing in what seems unshareable, of bringing community into what feels indelibly solitary. That's what I was focused on that fall as I trudged every weekday morning to the same coffee shop around the corner, lugging my stack of grief memoirs, taking care not to spill tea on my slowly growing pile of notes.

. . .

Around that time, the elder of my two children was turning five, and like many kids his age, he'd recently developed a fascination with and curiosity about death. My philosophy was to be as open and honest as possible without fueling any fires. "Answer questions directly, but don't dwell," was the advice my older sister, a mother of three, had given me a few years earlier, speaking of how to respond to those tricky questions that children inevitably ask as they learn about the world.

One of my friends was in the process of losing her mother to cancer, and she was helping her children anticipate that loss by sharing books on the subject. My child had gotten hold of one of these on a play date—the story of a boy whose goldfish dies—and since then he hadn't been able to stop talking about it.

"I'm dead now," he would sometimes say to me as we played games together, my invisible sword thrusting into his body, which would, in response, fall to the ground. "And now I'm not dead anymore," he would add a few seconds later, pulling himself up.

"Is *bubbeh* going to die?" he'd ask, referring to his ninety-something-year-old great-grandmother, whom we had at some point described as "very old" in an effort to explain why he had to be gentle around her, why he couldn't just jump into her lap as he wanted to. "Are *you* very old?"

I remember a family member, having overheard one of our many conversations on death, looking rattled. "Why are you talking to him about this?" she asked. "You're passing along your own personal obsession."

But the questions, the games, the curiosities had come from him. I was just responding to his queries, helping him work out what he was already so carefully churning in his mind.

. . .

Why would anyone voluntarily—even enthusiastically—submerge herself in death? "Early in my life, before anyone close to me had died," writes Edwidge Danticat in her recent meditation *The Art of Death*, "I was so afraid of death that I wanted to desensitize myself to it."[3] That, too, in the fall of 2016, was basically my line, though I would not have used the word *desensitize. I want to plunge into what scares me the most*, is what I might have said. *I want to be more aware of it, that other side of life.*

In many ways, what I wanted was to learn how to better see the grieving who are always among us, the grieving we will all, in one way or other, someday become.

Danticat continues, "Now that my father and mother and many other people I love have died, I want to both better understand death and offload my fear of it, and I believe reading and writing can help."[4]

I'm not sure that reading and writing about death has relieved me of my fears, but I do know that it makes me feel closer to those who have lost, those who are alone in their grief. It helps me begin to acknowledge their pain and suffering; in that way, it brings us nearer one another.

. . .

Reading about death so much of the time, I needed distractions. Dressing my kids in the morning and taking them together to drop the older one off at kindergarten, the younger one with a sitter; clearing away breakfast dishes; listening to podcasts on long walks through Prospect Park; thinking and talking with neighbors about the coming election. These were all suitable diversions, and they did the work of pulling me out of those endless, painful depictions of raw individual melancholy and loss. They returned me to the world.

In many ways, before Election Day, it was a season, too, of hopefulness, of a confidence often bordering on arrogance. Those talking heads on the radio and on TV and my own extensive but determinate social media circle: all were daily waxing on and on about how inevitable was Hillary's win. Even if not everyone was enthusiastic about it, even if many voiced reservations and regrets, it seemed like destiny, if only because the alternative felt so impossible.

Some days, when I had time to reflect, I could picture my childhood self marveling at a woman running the White House. I imagined my sons taking for granted that a woman could be—was—in charge of such an office. This had been something of a dreamlike hypothetical for me growing up, as for so many other little girls. Not that I would ever be president but that some woman could be.

"Of course girls can do anything boys can," my father had said to me often when I was young, pointing to Sandra Day O'Connor and eventually Ruth Bader Ginsburg as examples. He must have known that that was not really true, certainly not yet, but nevertheless he wanted to instill a confidence in me, that as a woman I would not feel bound by what I could not see, by what had or had not come before me.

Imagine a smart and competent woman perpetually in the public eye, making decisions, making mistakes, being put upon but enduring nonetheless. The thought was a comforting, if vague, abstraction—a diversion from the raw and individual stories of pain and grief I found myself marking up, day after day.

. . .

Every four years, a presidential election prompts so many publicized debates on civic and communal life that many Americans can't help but reflect on previous ones. But I have no memory of Obama's reelection in 2012. By November, my son was about to turn one after the longest year of my life. He was not, as I had quickly learned after a particularly long and painful labor, going to be one of those babies that parents brag about, the one who sleeps through the night at four weeks, who takes right away to sleep training or whatever tricks that miracle-working parent has in store.

I remember searching the Internet at some point in that first year to find out whether it was normal for my baby to cry throughout most of the day. My fears and concerns—Why won't he nap? Why does he always look so uncomfortable? Why can't he just get back to sleep?—intensified in the haze of sleeplessness and the suspicion I had that I was not going through a typical new mother experience. It would take years, a second baby even, to figure out how to confront my fears head-on, to recognize, after hearing so many other people's stories, that there is no such thing as a typical experience of parenthood, to learn how to share in the burden and confusion and not just in the elation and everyday small joys. Eventually, I became grateful for having a baby, later a young child, who knows how to ask for what he needs and who, if I can just stand to look, to listen, will help me help him.

"Why do people die, Mom?"

"I don't really have an answer. I just know that everyone, every living thing, dies at some point."

"Will I die?"

"Yes, but I hope not for a long time."

"Will you die?"

"Yes, but I also hope not for a long time."

"Will you die first?"

"I hope so."

. . .

There's another reason why that 2012 election, and indeed so much of what transpired back then, is such a blur. I was desperately attempting to finish graduate school and find a new job and figure out how to pay all the bills that were piling up in the wake of this new life. But everything came to a sudden halt that summer, when my son was only seven months old and we received a phone call telling us that a dear friend's young son, Finn, had died.

I was holding my baby when I got the news, and I remember my husband, Jon, taking him from my arms and putting him down, maybe in his playpen, maybe in his crib. I don't remember his crying, though, or mine, or Jon's; nor do I remember what we did with the baby when we went to the funeral—left him with the babysitter, perhaps. That summer, so hazy now in my mind, my life, our lives, felt like they had incontrovertibly split in two. Looking back, it still feels that way. Here was a loss I could not absorb; how does life go on in the wake of such tragedy?

I turned to books on grief and death for the first time, hoping to make sense of the impossible. What I have since learned was that nothing about that loss would ever make sense. Time would not heal.

But thinking back on Finn in life, talking about him with Jon and my sons, now makes me smile. I can still hear him singing along to Whitney

Houston the last time we visited and can still picture him carefully holding our new baby on his lap some months earlier, his grin huge. If I focus hard enough, I can remember the sound of his little kid voice calling out to his greatest love, the center of his world, "Mom. Mo-om."

Grief emerges because of love, because of life. Remembering Finn, in the company of those I love, produces joy.

. . .

On November 8, 2016, my husband and I eagerly rushed to the polls before school and work, with both kids in tow. We brought along a stroller, though our almost-two-year-old tried to pace alongside us for at least some of the ten-minute walk. The plot that would end with this Election Day denouement had been building; roles were clearly established. "Donald Trump is a bully, right?" our almost-five-year-old would often ask, and we would nod our assent. What else could we do but confirm this unnuanced but palpably accurate narrative he had carried with him home from school one day, along with his new art projects and emptied-out lunchbox? "We don't like him, right?"

Looking back, trying to reconstruct what feels, in retrospect, like an untraceable chain of events, I find that I took two photographs of our boys on that day: in one, their bodies are splayed across a gym floor, our voting site in Brooklyn. They look carefree, arms spread out, smiles wide. There are a couple of adult legs visible beside them, a line of people patiently waiting to vote. There are no traces of Jon's or my discomfort; our fears that this family excursion would end in tears, or tantrums, or worse, are not apparent in this snapshot. Because for our boys, of course, this was just another fun family excursion, albeit a rare opportunity to prance and play in the throes of a crowd, of people both familiar and strange.

In the second photograph, the kids are standing with their father, the younger one cradled in Jon's arms, a mischievous smile on his face, the older one standing and looking off to the side, his mouth slightly parted like he is mid-sentence. Jon is wearing an "I voted" sticker, even though he is also still holding a huge as-yet-unfilled ballot. My older one has an "I voted" sticker plastered on one of his cheeks. As I look at these photographs now, searching them for clues, the stickers look overly optimistic, boastful even. We should not have counted our chickens. We should have resisted a preemptive celebration, waited patiently for the time to come.

Returning home from the polls that day, we ran into neighbors and friends. The mood was light, our expectations already fixed. Soon after, we all went our separate ways; I returned alone to the cafe to dig into one of my memoirs of grief.

. . .

When I walked into my son's public-school kindergarten classroom the next morning, everyone looked glum. The teachers had set up plastic cups to fill with apple juice and spread cookies and treats across a table in honor of the expected celebration. In true kindergarten fashion—kids had to learn to be good sports, after all, and anyway a few parents in the class, it was rumored, were Trump supporters—this would remain a celebration. We sipped from our champagne glasses and made small talk. Each went her own way. Life, after all, had to go on.

In the weeks following, my older son woke up at night more often than usual, sometimes crying out from his bed to be soothed. It was something of a return to an earlier time, of more sleepless nights. I was adamant about not discussing the specifics of the election and its aftermath with him. We would go to a protest as a family, we would explain the basics of what was happening to neighbors and friends, but he had enough four-year-old worries to manage. Nonetheless, he absorbed our vibe, the adults talking in hushed voices about increased, sudden visits from ICE, our Muslim neighbors worrying that they could be deported.

In the wake of this unexpected result, my husband and I, like many others, searched for community. I found it in visiting with and talking to students and colleagues; he called his friends and family, debating what had gone wrong, what we could have done better. One night I received an e-mail from our local synagogue, inviting us to a postelection town hall, a time to mourn together. I was working, but my husband took the kids. Since both of our childhoods, our visits to synagogue had been relegated to using the swimming pool or, for him, playing in weekly basketball games at the gym. But in the weeks and months when we were adjusting to this new surreality, with Swastikas now daily appearing on synagogues and Jewish centers all over the country, we were willing to try new things, to reach out in alternative ways to the communities surrounding us. To find different ways of engaging.

. . .

Once the initial shock began to fade, some weeks after the election, I found that returning to my work, of all things, had become its own distraction. I started to parse the similarities and differences between the worn and angry faces of friends and neighbors, colleagues and students, and the haunting voices of the literature that I was reading. What's the connection between individual experiences of grief and communal ones? Are there ways to better see and be seen in our moments of loss, to somehow relieve one another, and accept relief, from the burdens of solitary grief?

The loss of an election, of a hope for a world where people are more willing to be held accountable for each other's pain and losses, starts off as a theoretical. Pretty soon, for so many, that initial abstraction turns into something very real: an experience confirming the knowledge that your body—and the bodies of people you care about—is not safe, that you are all alone in your own vulnerabilities. That every person's inevitable interdependence on others is something to be ashamed of, something to hide or disguise.

The loss of a loved one is, of course, anything but theoretical. It may take time, maybe even a lifetime, to come to terms with a death, but that loss is there in every minute of every day, in the spaces, now empty, of a shared home, in photographs, objects, and letters marking a history. There was a body, a look, a voice, a smile; now, only traces.

Still, there are points of convergence; while we were collectively losing an election, or while it was stolen through voter suppression and Russian interference, there were individuals starting, or continuing, to fade away, saying good-bye to one another in private, whispering and crying in hospital corridors and hospice beds. One loss does not preclude or slow down another.

Perhaps what a collective loss offers us is the potential, finally, to see each other across various modes and experiences of grief. If only briefly, in those weeks following the election, all of us who felt a loss were blinking through the intensity of a new, unanticipated day, our eyes unprotected, our pain and vulnerability plainly visible. That sudden transformation, that defeat, revealed to so many of us how quickly anyone can switch over into the grieving or the grieved.

It offers us, too, a chance to join forces, to act for each other as we concede that all of us are ultimately susceptible, however many layers of protection seem to divide us. How we are all, despite our varying everyday realities, at risk and reliant on one another. But we are also capable of transforming that dependence, that vulnerability, into a potent and unifying force, a way of moving forward, together, in the face of whatever comes next.

. . .

A month or so after the election, sometime in early December, I took my older son on some weekend excursion in Brooklyn. We chatted idly along the walk, as we usually do. Suddenly I found myself pulling on his arm, getting him out of the way so he would not step on a dead bird lying on the sidewalk.

We walked along in silence for a few minutes, his steps as lithe and restless as usual, until he finally said, "That was a dead bird."

"Yes, it was."

"That bird's not going to get up again, is it?"

I looked at him; something had shifted in the months since his obsession with death had peaked. Something, I realized, had finally sunk in.

"No, it's not."

We continued on for a few minutes, holding hands as we crossed busy streets, looking with amusement at the daily goings-on unraveling before us. Just as we walked onto our street, he paused again, suddenly serious.

"I feel sad about that bird," he said. "The bird who died."

I looked at his newly five-year-old face, a face I had seen grow and change so quickly. Sometimes, as now, his easy knowing, his ability to grasp the world, astonished me.

"I feel sad about that bird, too," I replied. And we charged home, having, for now, concluded our exchange.

NOTES

1. Joyce Carol Oates, *A Widow's Story: A Memoir* (New York: Ecco, 2012), 243.
2. Joan Didion, *The Year of Magical Thinking* (New York: Vintage, 2007), 74–75.
3. Edwidge Danticat, *The Art of Death* (Minneapolis, MN: Graywolf Press, 2017), 7.
4. Ibid.

WHEN WE SEE

KC Trommer

What is it to say I know you, you raised me, a man like you raised me?
     What does it matter that, because a man like you

raised me, I found other men like you and papered my life
with them? I know you. I have rid myself of you again and again.

What is it to watch you and all your tricks
but to not be able to warn the rest of them off of you?

What does it mean to listen, what does the sound of you beating inside our
     skulls mean, the sound of you so hard in us

that we stop being able to think of ourselves,
of what and who we love, with anything but fear?

Yes, I know you, I knew you, you are everything I have built myself
and my life away from, and here you are all over the radio, the television,

your name in everyone's mouth, the sound of a billion mouths forming your
     name, and even this I know because you are more known to me

than I am to myself, won't be enough for you—there is no enough.
What of it? This is the hope I'm tending to: that once we all have come to
     see

what it is you are and how you do what you do, that seeing it will be enough
     to end you. That seeing it will bring a great silence to you and men

like you. Silence—and the great space that your silence will make for the
     rest of us. That we will all see that you are not the story.

We are. We always were.

JUST TO GET BY

Bassey Ikpi

My father was the first to believe.

It began with a photo on the fridge. I was home from Brooklyn for a visit, poised at the ice dispenser, cup in hand. I saw the coffee-and-cream-colored man smiling down at me from the photo, a Redskins magnet just to the right of his head, his hand extended as though caught mid–high five, in that now-familiar presidential wave. I didn't recognize the face, but I'd spent enough time in Chicago to know the unusual collection of vowels and consonants that made up his name. What I didn't understand was what he was doing in our Nigerian-American home, tacked among old family photos and reminders to buy milk.

"Your father's boyfriend," my mother sniffed behind me, noticing my gaze, oil sizzling and bubbling around the plantain she was frying. "He donated to his campaign. Imagine. A whole senator in Chicago, and your father is here in Maryland giving him money. Why? I don't know." Her slight smile betrayed her clucking annoyance.

But that was my father. He tended to pick things up and invest in them even when it made sense to no one other than himself. It was terrible when it came to real estate, but his belief in people could warm you like a thousand summers.

Each visit home, there would be a new photo or a form letter written to feel personal.

"He wrote it to me, of course!"

We knew he was joking, but I knew how these things work. This is how politicians suck you in, how they make you feel invested in hope and change. But this was different. He was different, and that scared me more than anything. My father said over and over, "He is going to be the first black president."

We were never sure if he was joking. We tried to explain to him how these things work. Candidates want you to feel special, but it's just politics. And we didn't want him to become too invested. These people will disappoint. You can't trust them. If he were to ever run, white folks would never let him take office or live to see his term carried out.

. . .

A year later, I was in Brooklyn. Alone. A screaming newborn in my arms. Just days away from a surgery that would remove ten pounds of violent growth from my belly. My father called to check in on me. Our conversations had been stilted; once a "daddy's girl," I was now an embarrassment, something that placed shame on me: an unwed mother, a college dropout. He had invested in me, and I had disappointed him.

"Did you hear?" he asked, his voice quivering with excitement. "He's running for president! I knew it! He will win. I am telling you the truth."

I went home again a month later. By then, the number of photos on the fridge had grown, and my mother ordered them moved to his office. Week after week, there was an addition. This time a woman was added.

Michelle. She was beautiful but not in that way that made sense in this political Stepford world. You could tell by the way she held herself that she was just as much something as he was; you could tell by how he held her that she was everything.

This man and woman and those two beautiful brown girls. I began to sit with my father and watch the interviews and read the articles. And each week, another letter, another "personal" thank-you note, another photo. My father and I began a shaky climb back to each other as we discussed politics.

My father found joy in two things that tense year: his new grandson and this man who would be president. This Obama. Together they sat in front of the TV, this old man who was the first to believe and the child who embodied that belief, that the American dream was attainable.

"Obama! Obama! Yes, we can! Yes, we can!"

• • •

It's November 9, 2016, and my son is at the kitchen table poking at his breakfast. His body is crumpled and folded into the same heaviness that coats the world. The night before, I had sent him anxious and trembling upstairs to bed with the assurance that it was all going to be okay.

"Those states always go red. It's fine. It will all be fine in the morning."

And here it was: morning. And it was not fine.

His iPhone had already alerted him, and his morning was awash with tears and questions I did not have the language to answer. That same alert twisted me awake at 4:00 A.M.: "Donald Trump is the next president of the United States."

My son was quiet now, watching the syrup river spilling over his waffles. Every few minutes, he shook himself back into attention and forced a piece of food into a dry mouth. Any other day, there would be a scolding and urge to hurry up so he wouldn't be late for school. But today, I allowed the slow movements. I needed time to find answers and reassuring comments; I needed him not to worry. I needed him to hold on to the hope that was his whispered birthright. But I had nothing. I didn't know where to find it for myself, let alone have enough to hand it over.

In the car on the way to his school, the five-minute drive felt like it would go on forever. I kept the radio off to avoid any conversation about the election results. When we pulled up to the drop-off line at his school, we sat quietly and watched his red-and-khaki-uniform-clad classmates trickle into the building.

I searched my mind for something comforting. I rummaged through the words racing circles in my brain, hoping to come up with the perfect collection to make it all make sense and make it all better.

"It's going to be okay." It was boneless, but it was all I could manage. It was also not what I believed.

He nodded and gave one last sigh before he pushed his body against the door, dragging his backpack behind him.

"It's going to be okay," I offered again.

I whispered it to myself as I watched him join the mostly brown students filing into the small private school. One of us needed to believe it.

. . .

It's January 19, 2017. I find my father alone in front of the TV. There is a heaviness, a quiet louder than anything he's ever said. I know the answer but ask anyway: "Will you watch tomorrow?"

He shakes his head and points the remote toward the offending newcomer. As the TV clicks to black, he turns and walks away. I notice that his gait is slower—that pain in his hip—and I wonder if he heard me. As he passes me, leaned against the kitchen island, he responds: "I don't think I can."

He sighs, shrugs, and disappears into the hallway. He is headed to his office, to his computer filled with better news and his collage of photos collected over the years. Tacked among them are his grandson's honor roll and merit certificates.

This would not be an easy good-bye.

. . .

It's July. Congress has attempted to repeal health care several times. The hurricane of worry and hysteria that was created the first two times has settled into a quiet shrug.

My father, just home from an emergency hospitalization, rests on the couch, an MSNBC talking head listing the myriad ways millions will be affected if the law passes.

I'm in the kitchen, watching him as I've done since he's returned from the hospital. I wait to see his chest rise and fall a few times before I can exhale and turn to leave the room.

"If it happens, it happens."

"Pardon me, Dad?"

He raises himself off the couch and twists to face me. "I mean these people. We can't let them worry us so much. Every day, there's a new something. If it happens, it happens." He gingerly sits up and turns back to the faces on TV. His words calm me a bit. "If it happens, it happens."

There is a chaos of feet running down the hall, headed toward us. My son, home from soccer camp, runs in with a new card trick to show his grandfather.

"Grandpa!" he calls, just as the current president's voice fills the room; that voice makes me cringe like the squeak of Styrofoam pieces rubbing against each other do, and my instinct for months has been to leave the room. I've also taken to wearing wireless headphones around my neck to quickly drown out his voice when it becomes too much.

My son stops in his tracks. The eyes that already take up most of his face widen even further. I hold my breath for a second time, poised to rescue him at any sign of the anxiety or distress that have bubbled over the last few months.

Before I can suggest we turn the TV off, or send the boy on a fool's errand to get him out of the room, he turns to my father and quips, "I wish the Orange Menace would take a vow of silence." His grandfather's laugh rises above and drowns out the voice coming from the TV. His grandson comes up with a nickname as often as he can think of them: from the Fanta Fascist to Orangina Apocalypse.

My son loves the way his grandfather's mouth twitches and can barely get the jokes out before he breaks into his own laughter.

It took months to loosen the fear and worry that clung to the boy's thin frame. There is still work to be done to reclaim his once-quiet and black boy joy. Meanwhile, the old man's hope has taken a different shape—one that appreciates the slightly inappropriate jokes offered by a ten-year-old boy, one that welcomes resistance and resilience in the face of the uncertain.

I watch from the kitchen, marveling at the relationship between them. This is where my hope lives—in the way they hold each other, in the casual, loose way they are with each other. The laughter dies down, and the channel switches to the Cartoon Network. My father and my son are still draped over each other, this time conspiring against the 9:00 P.M. bedtime, the two of them folded into each other, their bodies bent and draped into an origami of whispers and giggles: delicate and beautiful.

To Ourselves

THEFT

Fran Wilde

—*For Mia*

That morning the officials
stole all the words.

We bit into apples sliced thin
and drank coffee, not noticing
that the table had disappeared,
the window
even as we talked and chewed and laughed.

Friends wrote columns of blank space
demanding a return
of sense and empathy

and the officials heard the
and saw the

Then they returned our words
in sacks. Gave them back
to us upside down.

So we sit at the thin
and sip at a table

And we bite into windows
The brittle glass stinging our tongues
and we refuse to stop chewing.

GASLIGHTING

Liana Finck

THREE DAYS

Ken Kalfus

First, the presidential campaigns seemed to go on forever, with thrills and spills and awfulness and scenes of obvious farce. Election night was gravely appalling. The immediate aftermath brought denial, bewilderment, and no small measure of grief—perhaps more grief than I've ever experienced in response to something in the news. In the months before the inauguration, some of us bargained with tragedy, trying to find signs that the man would accept the responsibilities of being president and give up the candidate's recklessness, but this hope quickly proved to be ungrounded in the reality of his character and the reality of the nation's politics.

His term began with a campaign of shock and awe—the immigration ban, for instance. Every day, so many standards of political behavior and political speech were overturned that they couldn't be absorbed. When we sat down to dinner or met friends in the street, we could speak only of our disappointment and our fear. We eventually had to change the subject. Then we became desensitized to the news, or bored by our tweet-sized thoughts, or enervated by the demonstrations of the president's ignorance, arrogance, and venality.

In his new pamphlet *On Tyranny*, Timothy Snyder cogently describes how past democracies have failed and how, in this present moment, they might fail again. A historian of twentieth-century Europe, especially the Nazi and Soviet dictatorships, Snyder emphasizes that those regimes' deliberate attacks on institutions, their degradation of language, and their devaluation of objective fact echo current "prefascist" American phenomena. He adds that in our era of television's continuously "breaking story," everything happens too fast to make sense of what's important. "The effort to define the shape and significance of events requires words and concepts that elude us when we are entranced by visual stimuli."[1]

The purpose of this essay's exercise is to stop briefly the blur of news that desensitizes, bores, and enervates. I want to seize a moment of political time—to slow it down, at least—and describe an ordinary three days in the life of the nation under the Trump administration, if only so that I will understand how these days were actually experienced before they became a segment in the arc of a longer history, given new meaning by future events. Months or years from now, this document may help me remember how things happened, as well as, of course, what I was thinking, correctly or not. These days have been selected for their convenience, nearly at random, lying between the completion of one project and my work on the next.

Wednesday, June 14, 2017

We wake this morning to news of a terrible fire in a London public housing tower—yet another calamity for the city in a season of calamities—but this is shortly superseded by breaking reports of a shooting in a public park in Alexandria, Virginia, on a ball field. A congressman and several congressional aides are seriously wounded. They're Republicans, practicing for the annual charity game against Democratic members and staff tomorrow night, a welcome vestige of bipartisan fellowship, though I suppose it would be even more bipartisan if they mixed the teams.

These horrific mass shootings are unpredictable in their targets but predictable in their frequency: every few weeks or so, at least when they're not presumed to be the almost-daily sprees related to criminal activity. (Last year there were more than fifteen thousand shooting deaths in the United States.) Our public response is predictable, too. The meaning of the attack, and even its moral weight, always depends on who did the shooting. We want to know the shooter's demographics, so we know which community to blame. Is he Muslim (a terrorist!) or white (a supremacist!)? It's also drearily predictable, and drearily valid, to say that the shooter is probably deranged and shouldn't have had access to the gun. The *New York Times* initially reports only that the shooter is "a man with white hair and a beard," a James Hodgkinson from Belleville, Illinois.[2] No demographics.

But, uh-oh, the *Daily Beast* has a picture of Hodgkinson and tweets that he "loved Bernie Sanders and hated 'racist & sexist' Republicans."[3] So this will be charged to our account.

President Trump, donning his usual rictus of glower, makes a statement at the White House, and it's managed appropriately, though not without a little hokeyness. He addresses the wounded congressman, Steve Scalise, and he's unable to resist his characteristic bombast and exaggeration: "And, Steve, I want you to know that you have the prayers not only of the entire city behind you, but of an entire nation and, frankly, the entire world."[4] The entire world? *Frankly?*

. . .

This morning's political commentary mostly concerns Attorney General Jeff Sessions's testimony to the Senate Intelligence Committee yesterday. The "General," as the senators called him, according to some obscure protocol, was forceful and slippery. When that didn't work, he stonewalled them, backed up by some of the Republicans. Sessions maintained that he recommended FBI director James Comey's dismissal because he poorly handled the Clinton e-mail investigation. No one asked if he was at least surprised when Trump told NBC's Lester Holt days later, "And in fact, when I decided to just do it, I said to myself—I said, you know, this Russia thing with Trump and Russia is a made-up story."[5]

The pundits' reviews of Sessions's performance are mostly negative, if not contemptuous. The *Times* editorial page observes that the attorney general mostly clammed up but was perhaps "wise to keep his mouth shut. When he opened it, he often seemed to contradict himself, his staff at the Justice Department, or the president."[6] Amy Davidson Sorkin at the *New Yorker* says the testimony "was by turns dismissive, incoherent, evasive, and shameful."[7] Doing some very modest due diligence, I also checked the *National Review*, where David French, usually a Trump critic, is "struck by the total lack of any compelling claims supporting the 'big' collusion narrative."[8]

Sure, there aren't any compelling claims, so far, especially if you limit the question of wrongdoing to a narrow, specific item and give Trump and his associates a pass on "small" collusion. Anyway, legal commentators are saying that collusion is hard to define and not a crime in itself. On the other hand, money laundering, accepting foreign assistance in an election, and obstruction of justice are criminal enough. When we fixate on collusion, we're setting ourselves a trap.

The week that Trump fired Comey, he confessed obstruction of justice not only to Lester Holt but to the Russians themselves in an Oval Office meeting from which American reporters had been barred. It seemed to me then that the president could not possibly remain in office: he would either be impeached or be forced to resign (while claiming that his presidency had been the biggest success in the history of the world, frankly). But at this writing it seems unlikely that he won't serve out his first term. The Republicans hold Congress. They don't seem to be suffering a political price for supporting him, even with the evidence of his criminality and unfitness for office laid out for all the world to see.

(Or am I saying this to jinx the unlikelihood of his departure? I want to be as wrong about this as I was when I predicted the outcome of the election.)

Tonight, the *Washington Post* reports that special counsel Robert Mueller appears to be investigating the obstruction charge. His office has requested interviews with intelligence officials who, according to published reports, were asked by Trump to intervene with Comey.[9] If these reports are true, the charge of obstruction would rise not from a single unguarded comment by a naive or demented elderly man but from evidence of a concerted campaign. Of course, I should be overcome by disgust and grief for the damage done to our republic. In truth, I'm delighted to see the man in legal jeopardy.

And by the way, the *Times* reports in a last paragraph, Mueller's also looking for evidence of money laundering, specifically an effort to hide Russian payments to Trump's associates through offshore banking centers.[10] Boy, is Trump going to be pissed.

Thursday, June 15, 2017

And he is! With the early morning dew, birdsong: "They made up a phony collusion with the Russians story, found zero proof, so now they go for obstruction of justice on the phony story" and "You are witnessing the single greatest WITCH HUNT in American political history—led by some very bad and conflicted people! #MAGA"

He probably doesn't mean *conflicted* in the dictionary sense of contending with opposing emotions—though it's conceivable that honest, patriotic, establishment-respecting prosecutors, some of them Republicans, do feel ambivalent about investigating the elected president. But Trump and his defenders are trying to undermine Mueller with specious conflict-of-interest charges and strong hints that he might be fired. Trump evidently wanted to fire him earlier in the week. His staff talked him down, warning of catastrophic political consequences. The inhibitory power of those warnings, however, has a short shelf life. Dozens of times, Trump has avoided adverse consequences for actions that would have brought down lesser politicians. And windbags like Newt Gingrich are still egging him on.

. . .

My concern yesterday that Democrats would be blamed for the Alexandria shootings was expressed almost as a joke, but in fact the question of whether liberal discourse is responsible dominates the day. The *Times* piece "Attack Tests Movement Sanders Founded" suggests that Hodgkinson was incited by Sanders's rhetoric. It's an unfair story. Here's the example of rhetoric in the lede: Sanders calls Trump a "demagogue" and "perhaps the worst and most dangerous president in the history of our country." Later in the story, Sanders is said to have "thundered" against the "extreme right-wing leadership in the U.S. House and the U.S. Senate."[11]

I can't see how this language can be characterized in any true way as incitement, or as militant, or as extreme. Without even citing the

Republican calumny directed at Barack Obama and the Clintons, we know that political debate in free countries has often employed charges of demagoguery and warnings of danger, and a politician is supposed to raise his voice. (I think Sanders is correct, too, but that's more contestable.) Partisan voices are now conflating Hodgkinson with all opposition to the president. The *Times* reports a tweet by the radio host Michael Savage: "I warned America the Dems constant drumbeat of hatred would lead to violence!"[12]

For now, at least, this attack isn't necessarily a harbinger of political violence by either side. But rhetoric from either side can inspire: that's the point of rhetoric. Men (almost exclusively) are easily inspired to warfare, and those weapons are out there, as abundant as every kind of human pain and every kind of human weakness, fixed in our minds as a solution to *something*.

Most Americans don't appreciate the true misery of nationwide civil conflict: the fear, the alienation, the ruined lives, and the death count on a scale beyond anything living generations have experienced. I lived in Yugoslavia in 1991 and 1992, the first year of the civil war, and I watched while lovely people in a charming land sealed themselves off in their own media bubbles and their own histories of victimization. That year has made me wary of intense political rhetoric, the kind that sees no communality with the other side, the kind that trades in provocative allusions to violent remedy. You can hear all sorts of extreme things among like-minded people anywhere, anytime.

One kerfuffle earlier this week centered on the Public Theater's upcoming Central Park production of *Julius Caesar*, in which the dictator is portrayed as a poofy-haired buffoon, his Calpurnia East European. Conservatives claimed the production was an incitement to murder. The Fox News chyron helpfully identified the show as an "NYC Play." The theater lost several corporate sponsors. Liberals, joined by Shakespeare scholars, explained that not only does the play not celebrate assassination; it's a tragedy that dramatizes how Caesar's killing lead to the dissolution of the Roman Republic.

Sure, I get it, but I also understand that the production portrays Trump as a tyrant fated to be put to death, his blood flowing copiously. Metaphors are mutable, outliving sixteenth-century connotations, and it's bad faith to argue that you haven't imposed a new meaning on something when it's clear you're straining to do just that. For centuries Serbs held up three fingers, a sign of the Trinity, to demonstrate their religious veneration, but in the prelude to the civil war, the gesture became a symbol of militancy. Non-Serbs were terrified; they found their own symbols of militancy—or maybe they found their symbols first, you never know. Ultimately, they went for their guns. In the early 1970s, the Confederate flag was considered a symbol of personal rebellion and the noncoastal counterculture, emblazoned on Alabama and Lynyrd Skynyrd album covers and the car driven by the Dukes of Hazzard. Then the flag was reclaimed by white supremacists as a token of racism and hate. Some of the Southerners who still maintain that the flag is no more than a symbol of Southern culture are sincerely oblivious; others are winking.

I love Shakespeare in the Park, and I would attend this production if I could, but let's not pretend some metaphors and symbols don't rouse us to violence.

. . .

The Republican-Democrat baseball game is played as scheduled, with patriotic spectacle and far more public interest than usual, including nearly twenty-five thousand spectators at Nationals Park, outdrawing five major league contests tonight. All the congressional leaders are there. The bipartisanship is played up. There's some kind of group prayer-hug before the game. One of the injured Capitol police, still bandaged and leaning on crutches, throws out the first ball.

I might be moved if I were in the ballpark, but I watch the game broadcast live on Facebook. Until the powers that be step in, the program is accompanied by a stream of public comments at the bottom of the screen that, in their eloquence and wisdom, make Twitter look like the Roman Senate, pre-Caesar. They suggest that the worthless congressmen should give their paychecks directly to charity, that the money is going to the Clinton Foundation, that the Democrats should move to Venezuela if they want socialism. I would guess the inanities are running 3–1 Republican, for those keeping score at home.

The Democrats win and give the trophy to the Republicans to put in Steve Scalise's office until he returns. The silenced commenters, and much of the public, probably find these gestures meaningless, but I think right now every little nudge toward national comity is worthwhile.

Friday, June 16, 2017

Meanwhile, in some alternate universe, on Earth II, they've been obsessed about North Korea for the past three months. What is President Clinton going to do? The regime has been test-firing missiles into the sea near Japan. Some can apparently reach the American West Coast, or they will soon have that capability, as well as the capability to deliver miniaturized nuclear warheads. Here on the Earth we actually inhabit, the president has paid fitful attention to the issue, counting on China, after a fun weekend with Xi Jinping at Mar-a-Lago, to pressure the North Koreans in exchange for a pass on trade issues. "There is a perception that the Chinese played to his vanity and fleeced him," said Christopher Hill, the former special envoy to North Korea.[13]

One also easily perceives that after the president's meeting with Xi, the Trump family was given several new business opportunities in China—so maybe he wasn't fleeced entirely. North Korea's latest test launch, of several land-to-ship cruise missiles, was June 7.

Otto Warmbier, an American student tourist held by North Korea, was returned home yesterday in a coma, which the North Koreans attribute to botulism. Doctors in Cincinnati who examined the young man say he suffered "extensive loss of brain tissue," the implication being that he was beaten.[14] This has not yet become a cause célèbre, as it has on the other planet, where Republicans are linking the president's failure to rescue Warmbier to her treason in Benghazi. There will be a congressional investigation.

Tragically, and way under the radar, both worlds are almost certain to be returning to a new era of mutually assured destruction. We can obliterate Pyongyang, but the North Koreans will be in a position to inflict unacceptable damage to American cities before our next presidential election comes around. The only way to manage this will be through normalization and negotiation, as it was the last time we met a nuclear adversary who seemed to be irrationally evil and brutally aggressive. American public opinion hasn't even begun to be prepared for normalization, as it was prepared for peaceful coexistence and then detente with the Soviets, thanks to frequent political summits, cultural exchanges, and popular media. In the 1960s and 1970s, Western television and film spies were always partnering with their Russian counterparts to save the world from a common enemy. Nothing like a North Korean–inflected version of *The Spy Who Loved Me* now seems remotely possible.

The casualties in the Grenfell Tower fire are now likely to exceed seventy, and public anger is rising, especially toward Theresa May, whose response is seen as uncaring and ineffectual. Comparisons have been made with post-Katrina Bush. Upon her arrival at the burned-out building, May is met with cries of "Coward!" and "Shame on you." Angry Londoners heckle Sadiq Khan, their mayor, too. The tower had no sprinklers, and it had been cheaply and possibly improperly clad. Not all the tenants have been accounted for.

One of the stories that came out of the fire: A four-year-old girl was dropped from a fifth-floor window and was caught by an onlooker, a man named "Pat," according to the *Telegraph*. Her mother is thought to have perished.[15]

The fire is turning into another demonstration of inequality and globalized wealth. London has actually done a better job than most of the world's cities in scattering public housing throughout the immensely prosperous capital. The upside is that poorer residents should have the same access to public services (police, schools) as the wealthy; the downside is that everyday inequality stares them in the face. The rich rely on private analogues to public services anyway: private security forces, private schools, and so on. Grenfell's twenty-four-story cinder will now hover above Chelsea for months, if not years, a monument to injustice.

Jeremy Corbyn, leader of the opposition Labour Party, has called for the newly made homeless to be allowed to occupy the vacant homes of the absent wealthy. These homes should be "requisitioned if necessary."[16] No word yet from the Russian oligarchs who have parked their money in British real estate.

• • •

Trump continues his campaign against the Justice Department. He tweets today, "I am being investigated for firing the FBI Director by the man who told me to fire the FBI Director! Witch Hunt." His tweet was the first official confirmation that he's a target of the investigation—after months of his trying to get the FBI to declare he's *not* a target of the investigation. Trump son-in-law and special advisor Jared Kushner is being investigated, too, according to a new story in the *Washington Post*, and Mueller has asked for the transition team's documents related to Russia and Ukraine. Mueller has also hired thirteen more attorneys. The special counsel seems to be moving fast—possibly in the event that he *is* fired. And, finally, it's apparent that the president doesn't know the meaning of the words *witch hunt*. In this situation, he should be more worried about a *fishing expedition*.

In his tweets, Trump goes after Deputy Attorney General Rod Rosenstein, who appointed Mueller, hoping to undermine or intimidate him and thereby derail the investigation. You have to wonder how often he got away with these tactics as a private businessman. But the Justice Department and the FBI are going to defend the prerogatives of their institutions. The *Times* reports that the president views Sessions and Rosenstein "less as executors of law than as salaried staff"[17]—apparently not only a frame of mind but also stunning ignorance.

Meanwhile, Trump loyalists like Gingrich and Sean Hannity rail against the pillars of the "deep state"—that is, the republic's institutional foundations. Together they're making a very conscious effort to go beyond obstruction and defeat the rule of law.

. . .

A jury in St. Paul today acquitted the police officer who shot Philando Castile last year, after the black motorist was pulled over for a broken taillight. His girlfriend, Diamond Reynolds, was in the passenger seat, and her four-year-old daughter was in the back seat of the car. Castile, a thirty-two-year-old cafeteria worker, calmly told the officer that he had a licensed gun before complying with an order to produce his driver's license. Then the officer shot him seven times. With preternatural presence of mind, Reynolds filmed the aftermath and live-streamed it on Facebook, providing vivid commentary for a worldwide audience.

I haven't been following the trial, the police haven't released their own dash-cam video, and it's hard to know what was in the jurors' minds, but the circumstances seem pretty clear. The officer (who's Latino) pulled Castile over without good cause. He panicked when he saw the gun, even though Castile first alerted him to it. He operated with reckless disregard, especially with Reynolds and her child in the car. The circumstances have been clear in many of the high-profile police killings of black men, also captured on video, that have roiled the nation in the past couple of years. A *Times* list of fifteen similar shootings includes two that have resulted in convictions of police officers.[18]

What's new isn't the police misconduct, of course, but the video technology, in every pocket and in every purse, potentially always on, potentially always a finger-tap away from dissemination. As was said in 1992 after the police beating of Rodney King was caught on video, *we're watching Big Brother*—but that hasn't led to more civil liberty or more civil security.

The omnipresent camera can also expose humanity and extraordinary grace and real love. That, too, is part of the media blur. I rewatch the videos several times. After the shooting, Reynolds is handcuffed (*why?*) and put in the back of a police car with her daughter. Another camera, mounted in the car, is filming her now. Reynolds becomes momentarily distraught. Four-year-old Dae'Anna offers her comfort: "It's okay. I'm right here with you." Then she tenderly embraces her. She adds, "Mom, please stop cussing and screaming 'cause I don't want you to get shooted."[19]

. . .

The *Julius Caesar* flap turns out to have legs. During tonight's performance, the third act is interrupted by a well-known conservative activist who rushes onto the stage as the tyrant is being stabbed. "Stop the normalization of political violence against the right!" she cries. "This is unacceptable!" Her performance is filmed by another activist, who shouts, as security people lead them both from the theater, "You are Goebbels. . . . You are inciting terrorists. The blood of Steve Scalise is on your hands!" The play resumes, to a standing ovation, at the line, right after "Et tu, Brute," when one of the conspirators announces, "Liberty! Freedom! Tyranny is dead!"[20]

The Public Theater tweets, lamely, that the activists are "paid protesters." This is, of course, what the president has said about those who have marched against him. I'm glad there are so many new job opportunities!

I'm not sure how the disruption of a provocative theatrical event is so much different from the commotions brought by left-wing activists who have shouted down visiting college speakers—many of whom have come to campus intending to provoke that exact response. Both sides want the drama. Both sides want to show how aggressive they can be. And both whine, "The other side started it!" Tit-for-tatism is among the most pernicious of human doctrines, whether in our personal relationships or in our public affairs. I presume that disruptions of public events will now intensify—at shows, at politically themed readings and concerts, at lectures, and, of course, at campaign rallies. And someone will bring a gun.

Notes

1. Timothy Snyder, *On Tyranny: Twenty Lessons from the Twentieth Century* (New York: Tim Duggan Books, 2017), 61.

2. Michael D. Shear, Adam Goldman, and Emily Cochrane, "Congressman Steve Scalise Gravely Wounded in Alexandria Baseball Field Ambush," *New York Times*, June 14, 2017, available at https://www.nytimes.com/2017/06/14/us/steve-scalise-congress-shot -alexandria-virginia.html.

3. See the *Daily Beast*'s Twitter post of June 14, 2017, at 8:50 A.M., at https://twitter .com/thedailybeast/status/875017536714272768?lang=en.

4. Donald Trump, "Statement by President Trump on the Shooting in Virginia," June 14, 2017, available at https://www.whitehouse.gov/briefings-statements/statement-president -trump-shooting-virginia.

5. Donald Trump, interview by Lester Holt, *Nightly News with Lester Holt*, May 11, 2017, available at https://www.nbcnews.com/nightly-news/video/president-trump-this -russia-thing-is-a-made-up-story-941962819745.

6. "Jeff Sessions Clams Up in Congress," *New York Times*, June 13, 2017, available at https://www.nytimes.com/2017/06/13/opinion/jeff-sessions-clams-up-in-congress.html.

7. Amy Davidson Sorkin, "Jeff Sessions and the Trail of Unanswered Questions," *New Yorker*, June 14, 2017, available at https://www.newyorker.com/news/daily-comment/jeff -sessions-and-the-trail-of-unanswered-questions.

8. David French, "The Big Collusion Narrative Keeps Melting Down," *National Review*, June 13, 2017, available at https://www.nationalreview.com/blog/corner/big-collusion-narrative-keeps-melting-down.

9. Devlin Barrett, Adam Entous, Ellen Nakashima, and Sari Horwitz, "Special Counsel Is Investigating Trump for Possible Obstruction of Justice, Officials Say," *Washington Post*, June 14, 2017, available at https://www.washingtonpost.com/world/national-security/special-counsel-is-investigating-trump-for-possible-obstruction-of-justice/2017/06/14/9ce02506-5131-11e7-b064-828ba60fbb98_story.html.

10. Michael S. Schmidt and Matt Apuzzo, "Mueller Seeks to Talk to Intelligence Officials, Hinting at Inquiry of Trump," *New York Times*, June 14, 2017, available at https://www.nytimes.com/2017/06/14/us/politics/mueller-trump-special-counsel-investigation.html.

11. Yamiche Aclindor, "Attack Tests Movement Sanders Founded," *New York Times*, June 14, 2017, available at https://www.nytimes.com/2017/06/14/us/politics/bernie-sanders-supporters.html.

12. Ibid.

13. Mark Lander, "As Trump Bets on China's Help on North Korea, Aides Ask: Is It Worth It?" *New York Times*, June 15, 2017, available at https://www.nytimes.com/2017/06/15/world/asia/china-xi-jinping-trump-north-korea.html.

14. Susan Svrluga, "Otto Warmbier Has Extensive Loss of Brain Tissue, No Obvious Signs of Trauma, Doctors Say," *Washington Post*, June 15, 2017, available at https://www.washingtonpost.com/news/grade-point/wp/2017/06/15/otto-warmbier-has-extensive-loss-of-brain-tissue-no-obvious-signs-of-trauma-doctors-say.

15. "'Hero of Grenfell Tower' Caught Four-Year-Old Girl 'like a Rugby Ball' after She Was Thrown by Mother from 5th Floor," *The Telegraph*, June 16, 2017, available at http://www.telegraph.co.uk/news/2017/06/16/hero-grenfell-tower-caught-four-year-old-girl-like-rugby-ball.

16. "London Fire: Corbyn Calls for Empty Flats to Be Requisitioned," *BBC News*, June 16, 2017, available at http://www.bbc.com/news/uk-politics-40285994.

17. Michael D. Shear, Charlie Savage, and Maggie Haberman, "Trump Attacks Rosenstein in Latest Rebuke of Justice Department," *New York Times*, June 16, 2017, available at https://www.nytimes.com/2017/06/16/us/politics/trump-investigation-comey-russia.html.

18. Jasmine C. Lee and Haeyoun Park, "In 15 High-Profile Cases Involving Deaths of Blacks, One Officer Faces Prison Time," *New York Times*, December 7, 2017, available at https://www.nytimes.com/interactive/2017/05/17/us/black-deaths-police.html.

19. Melissa Etehad, "'I Don't Want You to Get Shooted': Philando Castile Video Shows Reaction of Girlfriend's 4-Year-Old Daughter," *Los Angeles Times*, June 22, 2017, available at http://www.latimes.com/nation/la-na-video-diamond-reynolds-daughter-20170622-story.html.

20. Michael Paulson, "Two Protesters Disrupt 'Julius Caesar' in Central Park," *New York Times*, June 17, 2017, available at https://www.nytimes.com/2017/06/17/theater/julius-caesar-central-park-trump-protesters.html.

TERROR? WHAT IS TERROR?

Liana Finck

FOUR STORIES ABOUT FIGHTING

Sandra Newman

One of my earliest memories is of a war between girls and boys, fought
during recess periods at my elementary school. I remember only odd
moments from it: crouching behind a low stone fence with some sort of
projectile in my hand; being caught on a jungle gym by a boy who tagged
me and screamed in agony, "Girl cooties!"; charging pell-mell across a field
with a band of eight-year-old comrades, shouting a battle cry. The war
extended over several recess periods until it felt like a part of life—the most
central, crucial part of life. Through all those days, I was making believe
that winning this war would change the world. It's one of my happiest
memories.

The point of this story is that political violence is exhilarating
whether or not it serves any purpose. It doesn't appeal to just zealots and
psychopaths; it's something even children love. We're predisposed to
imagine that violence will be more effective than nonviolence, even though
that's generally false.

Of course, most of us agree that there are times when the fate of the
world depends on our willingness to employ force, when the end justifies
the means. But the fate of the world more commonly depends on our ability
to refrain from violence under great provocation. It may even depend on
our willingness to sacrifice our lives without striking out against those who
oppose us.

As I write this, a woman has just been killed by a white supremacist
terrorist at the Unite the Right protest in Charlottesville, Virginia. The
organizer of that protest, Jason Kessler, was chased away by an angry mob
while trying to give a press conference. In a remarkably short period of
time, we've arrived at a point where people who always assumed they would
live their lives in peace are wondering whether political violence is justified,
and under what circumstances.

Here I tell four stories directly or indirectly about violence, which I
hope may illustrate some of the complexities involved in such decisions.
In order, they address defusing the threat of violence, violence as political
theater, violence as retaliation, and the senseless violence that can arise as
a result of political violence. I present the stories without commentary, but
I preface them here by saying they shouldn't be taken as an argument for

or against any course of action. Rather, they're invitations to thought. If one of these stories makes you feel approval, why? If one makes you angry or uncomfortable, why? What do your reactions tell you about your beliefs about violence and nonviolence?

The First Rodeo

Roughly twenty years ago, my friend Stanley went on a trip to Montana. While he was there, the friend he was visiting took him to see a rodeo. At that time, Stanley had a Jewfro of about four feet in circumference, a stunning object the size of a full-grown sheep.

After the rodeo, they went to the rodeo bar, and Stanley's friend went to the bathroom, leaving Stanley alone. Immediately, he found himself surrounded by seven rodeo guys. One guy (described by Stanley as a "steer-wrassler") slowly took out a knife. He opened it up and said, "A man came through here a couple weeks ago with long hair like that. I had to give him a haircut with a rusty blade."

Then all the other rodeo guys glared at Stanley threateningly.

Stanley said very nicely to the steer-wrassler, "Wow, I would love to get a haircut. But if I did, I would lose my job."

The rodeo guys were flummoxed. The steer-wrassler said, "Job? What kind of a job is that?"

Stanley said, "I'm an actor. I just made the first half of a film, and in two weeks I have to go back to New York and make the second half. So I can't cut my hair."

The steer-wrassler said, "Can I touch it?"

The Crazy Friend

My friend Will and his "crazy friend" Jesse were in Amsterdam at a bar, sitting in the outdoor section at the side of a canal. It was a beautiful summer day, but their enjoyment of it was being spoiled by a man talking loudly on his cell phone. This was at a time when cell phones were still an accessory for rich businessmen, so in addition to being annoying, this behavior had an undercurrent of class warfare.

The instant the man got off his phone, Jesse went up to him and said, "Can I see your phone for a second? I want to show you something amazing."

The man was naturally reluctant, but Jesse kept insisting that it was an amazing trick, and it wouldn't harm the phone, and it was really amazing. Finally, with some trepidation, the man gave Jesse the phone. Jesse instantly handed it to Will. Then he caught the man in a big bear hug and, holding him to his chest with a grip of iron, jumped into the canal.

The Cigarette

One day, when I was twenty-two years old, I was sitting on a park bench in shorts, smoking a cigarette. A man passing by muttered something to me and bent down and stroked my thigh. Then he kept on walking as if it was nothing.

This was not my first experience of sexual assault, or even my fifth or sixth, and I was filled with a rage out of all proportion to the crime. I got up and chased the man and put my cigarette out in his ear. He shrieked in pain and turned and shouted at me. I grimaced at him as if to say, "That's what you get, groping man," and stalked away. He didn't attempt to follow me, which was probably good for both of us.

When I look back on this, I can't say it was the right thing to do. However, whenever I remember it, I'm filled with unalloyed joy.

The Sailor

The last story is told by Serge Lifar, the former ballet master of the Paris Opera Ballet, in his memoir, *Ma Vie.* Lifar grew up in Kiev at the time of the Russian Revolution, when the city was repeatedly taken and retaken by four different armies. Kiev had fallen into perfect anarchy; the boundary between crime and lawfulness had completely vanished.

One evening during this time, the young Lifar was at a concert hall watching a marksman's act. The performer, in formal evening dress, was firing a pistol at his wife, who, of course, was never harmed by the bullets. Lifar tells us, "Sitting next to me was a young sailor, a very good-looking lad with bare chest. He wore only sailor's trousers and a jacket that did not hide his tattoo-marks. On his head was a little hat and he had on his arms a number of gold bracelets. He sat staring at the stage . . . apparently fascinated by the act. Suddenly he pulled out his revolver and, as though to prove whether the apparent miracle was a real one or not, he shot the woman dead. The crowd did not budge, it seemed stupefied, while the sailor, his eyes quite expressionless, seemed little by little to realize what he had done. Finally, in nightmare silence, he got up and left the hall."[1]

NOTE

1. Serge Lifar, *My Life*, trans. James Holman Mason (London: Hutchinson, 1965), 14.

THE ACCUSED BY KHUN SRUN

Madeleine Thien

The angel of history, in Walter Benjamin's famous description, is propelled backward into the future as the storm of progress accumulates before his eyes. Benjamin remarks on how the angel "would like to stay, awaken the dead, and join together what has been smashed to pieces" but cannot withstand the force of the storm.[1]

As I try to write about the storm of history now before us, I am haunted by the work of the Cambodian writer Khun Srun. Through novels, poetry, and essays, Khun examined how a person could live a moral life in a time of devastating, and escalating, violence. He posed the questions that Immanuel Kant believed encapsulated the deepest humanity of an individual: *What can I know? What should I do? What may I hope?*

The Cambodian conflict, a proxy war that involved the United States, Russia, and China, began in 1965. By 1973, Cambodia, the sideshow to the war in neighboring Vietnam, was the most heavily bombed country in history. The United States, in order to pursue its Vietnamese targets, dropped 2,756,941 tons of bombs on Cambodia, a country with which it was not at war; in fact, Cambodia's military government was allied to, and received funding from, the United States. For Cambodia, a small country no larger than Missouri, the result was catastrophic. In the ensuing famine and horror, ordinary people turned to the Communist resistance, the Khmer Rouge. Scholars Ben Kiernan and Taylor Owen report in *The Walrus*, "Civilian casualties in Cambodia drove an enraged populace into the arms of an insurgency that had enjoyed relatively little support until the bombing began."[2]

Khun's last novel, *The Accused*, published in 1973, is narrated by a writer imprisoned by Cambodia's U.S.-backed military government. The accused asserts that he is not a person of politics or even a man of conviction but simply an observer and a writer. He, a lover of literature, wants to flee the country and be part of the wider world; yet he is driven to live a life of principle. Shortly after *The Accused* was published, Khun left Phnom Penh and joined the insurgent Khmer Rouge.

In 1975, the Khmer Rouge, victorious against the military government, began a merciless purge of all suspected internal enemies and "impure" citizens. In December 1978, Khun, like so many who had committed their lives to the progressive ideals of the revolution, was arrested. He was held in the school where he once taught mathematics and which had become the most notorious prison of the regime. Days after his arrest, Khun, his wife, and three of his children were executed. Only Khun's nine-year-old daughter survived, taken by the Khmer Rouge and forced to flee with them. Two weeks after Khun's execution, the Khmer Rouge fell from power. By then, 1.7 million Cambodians, fully one-third of the country's population, had died in the neglect, starvation, and purges of the regime.

The Accused is a book of questions. It is a disquisition on war, folly, and death and, most of all, on his desire to live. It reads like a prayer. He was twenty-eight years old when he published it.

Observing the United States and other nations today, I fear the world we are unleashing. Was the age of confrontation and its righteous violence, its hall of mirrors, inescapable for Khun Srun? If people had refused to believe that others were political or ideological enemies, that the brutalization of language had no consequence, that salvation in the form of a populist leader was at hand, that justice could be bought with wholesale destruction of what came before, that violence once unleashed could be contained—if those ideas had been refused in Khun Srun's Cambodia, and in the America that illegally bombed a neutral country, would anything now be different?

Am I a coward, Khun Srun wondered, to believe in nonviolence?

Khun Srun was failed by those in power in Cambodia and America, who, purposefully and cynically, made a complete laughing stock of legal protections. Totalitarianism's disregard for truth, Hannah Arendt wrote, is driven by the political conviction that not only is everything possible, but in a totalitarian world, everything is permissible.[3]

To commit, with honesty, to equality before the law while choosing nonviolence requires strength in numbers, superhuman commitment, and a letting go of our romanticized deification of warfare. Perhaps this is the radical democratization that the majority has never truly attempted: risking ourselves, putting everything on the line, to gain power not for our own ideologies but for the center. By center I mean not the center of power but the center where divergent and even incompatible ideas meet. A place in which, potentially, we are looking not for victory but for something that totalitarian forces, of the Left and Right, dismiss as comically foolish, naive, and cowardly: passionate thinking, which, to use Arendt's words, might be imagined as "judgment without scorn, truth-finding without zeal."[4]

No matter our political ideology, gender or sexuality, race or ethnicity, age or income, our lives are inextricably bound together: my freedom and safety depend on your freedom and safety. In countries that are truly free—where viewpoints clash, where multiple ways of being coexist—no ideological faction can take full control, except by violence.

Khun Srun knew that there must be other ways. He wrote, "I would like to discuss. I would like to oppose. / I would like to remove these walls and live as I have heard it is possible, without the imposition of their rules. / But what am I but a grain of dust?" Who made him the grain of dust? Was it the government and prevailing powers? Or was it all of us, his fellow human beings?

Fragments from *The Accused*, by Khun Srun

Khmer to French translation by Christophe Macquet
Translated from the French by Madeleine Thien

I still fail to understand.

I was born human.
Without having asked to be born.
Without having asked for a new existence.

I was born in a beautiful house.
I grew up in a comfortable family, enjoying a privileged place in society.
Things came easily to me: I ate and slept well. What I wanted I could buy.
     I could study and amuse myself. I did not face the obstacles that most
     boys my age must overcome.

Soon, I will go on a journey overseas.[5]

I was born empty and naked.
The infants around me: they, too, were born empty and naked.
I was lucky enough to meet good parents.
That's all.
Others drew an unlucky number.
All before we saw our first light.
If we exchange the wombs, we exchange the destinies.

And so we arrive, taken from the bodies of different mothers.
One child weeps: his mother is loving and attentive.
The other also weeps: his mother, just after giving birth, holds the child to
     her hip and continues her labor of misery.

The first already has a car, a house, people busy around him.
The other lives in a hut, torn by hunger, at the mercy of the sun, weather,
    mosquitos. As a child, he will carry cords of firewood or tend the oxen,
    without the chance to cross the doorway of a school.

. . .

I have the feeling of living between walls.
Ever since I reached the age of reason.
To live in ways I have not chosen.
Part of a society I did not choose.
I feel locked up.
I want to go out.
But I cannot leave.

These walls surrounding me are their laws, their police, their prisons, their
    guns.
Walls are their business, trade, and profit.
All that subjugates people.
All that reduces them to the rank of objects.

I would like to discuss. I would like to oppose.
I would like to remove these walls and live as I have heard it is possible,
    without the imposition of their rules.
But what am I but a grain of dust?

What to do?
Accept the routine?
Morning, noon, and night.
For years and decades.
Remain hanging on a nail.
Why?
To be happy, to be held in regard, to live in safety.
But this kind of happiness, how does it bring me happiness?
So that in the sum of things, I do not even know who I am. . . .

How is my life any different from those around me?
I see only the same faces, vacillating in the same way.
And if I ask the question, "What is the human being?"[6] they build a new
    wall before me: "Don't ask such questions. It's useless."
And yet, because it is a question of paths, the question is essential.
"Utility" is not the point.

One's humanity must also be the willingness to address this question: "What is the human being?"

. . .

Night. The moon, a quarter full, visible behind the bars of the prison window, shines more brightly than on previous nights.

I remember myself, a little boy at the pagoda. I remember myself, seated, bowed, both legs folded alongside my body, in the company of classmates who have since disappeared from my life. Nearby, a half-dozen monks rest; nearby, two or three candles and a few sticks of incense diminish, releasing thick curls of smoke. I prostrate myself from time to time, palms pressed together, before the smile and serenity of my teachers.

I know it is dangerous to live among men. I have known it for more than twenty years, ever since I reached the age of reason.

But twenty years ago, I never felt terror as I feel it now. Never.

The inspector interrogates me from every possible angle before rising, brutally, and moving to the cupboard beside me. A grand cupboard, solid and heavy, which had assessed me with a sinister and oblique gaze. What is the inspector reaching for? What will he withdraw? My heart hammers. I think of a train in the night. I am trembling everywhere. My lungs burn. My hands and feet are ice. I try to suppress my fear, but my nerves will not obey the dictates of my mind. Abruptly, an old expression comes to me: to piss myself from fright.

A kind of hope remains. Microscopic. I know that I am innocent and falsely accused. So I try to change my thoughts; I try to be hopeful: the inspector is Khmer, he has the same dark skin and the same blood as me.

Will someone let my mother know? Of this, they say nothing. She lives far from this place. Still, I've been dreaming of her. So I am no different from the other prisoners. Our nights are identical. We are all people of laughter, tears, and nightmares.

In my dream, my mother no longer wears her familiar smile. She is gaunt, and her hair is gray. Panic-stricken, she holds my eldest daughter by the hand. She hurries forward, gripped by a single desire: to secure me in her arms with all the force of her love, with all the clumsiness of too long an absence . . . but she is blocked by a guard who forces her to stop and go back. She looks at me for a long time without moving until at last she says to me in a frail voice, choked by sobs, "My child, what have you done?"

My daughter, she, too, gazes at me. Her small hand beckons, as if she were trying to tell me, *Come home.*

Her gesture shatters me, and I wake with a start, my eyes filled with tears.

I want to rejoin them, to embrace them, but in this place where I remain, all I can hold is the night.

I am freed on September 6 at 1 P.M. I say good-bye to everyone, even the guards. Too much joy! My feet barely feel the ground. I have the dreamlike impression of having been released from an examination, a trial.

. . .

I do not want to die.
If I did not mind, my problem would be easily solved.
No need to wait for an illness to chip away at my bones or a curse to
    befall me.
But I am desperate with alarm.
And shame.

Nobody wants to hand back the last breath.
But where to turn for help?
Who to call for aid?
The gods?
Beg them to deliver us?
It would be better not to depend on them.
Who even knows if they exist! No one has ever laid eyes on them.
Even our Minister of Security cannot be assured of his own security.

Some believe that only art and philosophy can take on death and win.
So perhaps I must become a great writer, poet, or grand philosopher, like
    Hugo or Rousseau, like Sartre, Camus, or Krâm Ngoy.[7]
Or the 3 M's: Marx, Mao, Marcuse.[8]
Or an exceptional statesman, like Napoleon, De Gaulle, Jayavarman VII.[9]
That's the way to make light of death, they say.

But all those men are dead; they die.
If only they could have lived a hundred years, two hundred, a thousand,
    even more.

And me, like them, eternal.
And all the others with us.

No one leaves this passage, this pitiless cycle of birth and disappearance.
And so I ask: Why continue to give life, if to give life is to give death?

Ever since I was a child, I have been obsessed by death.
What will become of my eyes? My ears, my heart, my lungs?

The gorge opens in me.
One day my eyes will no longer see.
One day my ears will no longer hear.
One day my heart will no longer beat.
One day my lungs will no longer breathe.
One day soon to come, all that is mine will be taken by the void.

So I ask this question. I shout this question with more and more strength:
    Why?

For the last year or two, I've had the impression of a tomb surrounding me
    in every direction.
It does not stop.
I picture my corpse.
They are taking me.
They are burying me.
They are burying the hands that are no longer my hands, the skin that is no
    longer my skin, the heart that is no longer my heart.
But why must it be dissolved?
Why must it be crossed out, for good, from the surface of the earth?

I remember so many honest people, devoted to the cause of the wretched,
    who passed on in silence.
Fallen into anonymity.
If only I could revive them!
But I do not know how. . . .

How many philosophers have tried to contain this ontological aporia?
In vain, they assessed the problem from every angle.
No remedy.
No way to escape the grand somersault.
Carefully, they concluded that we should not dwell too long on this and
    instead busy ourselves with other things.

And meanwhile, as they discourse, we take each other's lives.
Look at us.
Look at how we cut throats, how we slaughter.
It will never finish.
Such energy!
But to what end?
Taking life never made a man immortal.

If I die today, at this hour, what will happen?
My books will disappear.
They will bury me, despite my wishes, but what does it matter, since I will
    not be conscious?
Will I be a soul drifting above the earth's matter?
Or reincarnated into another existence?
They will speak of me, for a moment, and then they will forget me,
    because in the end the living always forget those with whom they do not
    interact.
Little by little, my wife and my daughter will forget, just as I forgot, bit by
    bit, the dead in my family.
That is how it is.

Death. A severed line.
Some friends will not even come to see my remains.
That is how it is, death and its reality.

And also, the hospital.
You must go through it.
From outside, you don't see.
From outside, we don't know.

I went in recently to bring emergency donations to the wounded.[10]
In the hospital, quotidian death.
Here, in all likelihood, is where we will finish one day.

Here, in the hospital, the same scream of horror floods my chest. A
    confusion of pain and refusal: It is not possible! It is simply not
    possible!

It is not possible that people are carved up so that other people can mend them.

All the bodies shredded. Amputated. All the infirmity. This sound of
    whimpering.

But is it not I who whimpers?
Is it not I who am too sensitive?

It could be that the majority do not have compassion for others.
They are consumed by their own existence and unbothered by the rest.
I had to rush from the room of amputees, because I could not bear the
  spectacle.

Poor Kakey,[11] abandoned on a raft in the middle of raging waves.
Immensity of the ocean.
Immensity of her despair.

Poor Meursault,[12] locked in his cell, analyzing his life from beginning to
  end, awaiting his execution.

But these are only characters.
Conjured by writers.
They are not real beings, facing their certain extinction.

We must turn to those who are condemned to death.
Those to be shot in the first light of morning.
Like Lieutenant-Colonel Tom Saravan.[13]
Like the dozens of political prisoners riddled with bullets, killed four or five
  years ago, at the end of Sihanouk's regime.[14]
Were they terrified? Did they have the urge to laugh? Did they regret their
  past? What came into their minds?
At the moment when they were bound, or blindfolded, or lined up against
  the wall.

A death sentence.
We must turn to those who lived through a mock execution.
What did they feel? Did a part of them die?
Did they then experience an unsurpassed joy?
They alone can tell us something of dying.

Now I wonder at the old, the terminally ill, those undergoing a last,
  desperate operation.
Are they afraid?
And where does their fear go?

I think of the young who do not fear death, because they are full of vigor,
  because they have lived only a little and do not realize how terrible the loss.

Of the young who are used by every revolution.
Of the young whom every revolution sends into combat, at the front lines,
    because they are more effective than the old.
I think of those who are maneuvered like pawns on the battlefields.
Of those who, obeying orders, sacrifice their lives.
I think of the Japanese kamikazes.
I think of the suicide bombers.
I think of the Jews, poor scapegoats, murdered in the millions.

The fear is great when one realizes that the last hour has arrived.
Perhaps the poet's fear is even greater, because emotions are highly
    concentrated in him; because he saw, when the world did not yet see,
    that the situation was without possibility.

But let us listen to the wise, like Comrade Tum,[15] whose hands were tied
    behind his back. He counseled us to banish fear. Fear is what causes
    people to hand over their souls.

    . . .

Death is a terrible thing. Therefore, does a man, in his turn, have the right
    to exact revenge?
I reply no.
He does not have the right.

Beautiful statement of the Universal Declaration of Human Rights.
Recognizing the inalienable rights possessed by every person, even the most
    miserable.
Banning torture. . . .
But we continue, undaunted, to beat, to persecute, to deprive others of their
    rights.
The dominant, above all, the rich, the guardians of capital, who, by
    cunning and constraint, use the labor of the wretched, the nobodies,
    and subdue them, constrict them, crush them like lice. . . .

And now we arrive at the origin of life's struggle.
It is almost a biological response.
To live.
To have dignity.
To not be crushed.
Without having to beg repeatedly for clemency or pity or mercy.
To struggle to live.
And then, to die.

Dying by one's beautiful death.
To not end, crushed by others.
And so to conquer life.
And so to conquer death.

Be happy.
Fight for this.
And then prepare to go on.
There are different ways.
Some try to gather to them everything they have loved in this life, their
  treasured belongings, their friends, all that gave them joy and pleasure.
Others, on the contrary, seek to divest themselves of everything, to let go
  of each attachment to this world, so as not to leave anything that will
  continue in pain.
They will leave only their skin and bones.

In *Matryona's Place*, by Solzhenitsyn, Matryona owns nothing.
Why accumulate property, she thinks, only to live in constant fear of being
  dispossessed?
That is my view as well.
I want to own neither house nor land, or riches of any kind, because I know
  that these goods will become so many useless attachments at the hour of
  leaving this world.
How much better to lead a simple existence.

But I will not universalize my position.
This would be an error.
Many others can find happiness in belongings.
I believe we each must disentangle life as best as we can.
The paths have no solution, but they are multiple.

In any case, we all find ourselves, one fine day, at the same point of waiting.

  * * *

I must choose between the path of wisdom and the path of desire, between
city and countryside, between Cambodia and the world, between the
present situation and a future I must make for myself. In short, to stay or
to go. I must choose. No one can do it for me. And I will be responsible for
my choice.

I think of my aging mother. I think of my little room. I think of my writing
desk, the cupboard I opened to take out my books, the chair on which I sat.

I think of my family, friends, loved ones. Their faces smile at me. My lips return their smile. A courgette soup with anchovies brings me pleasure. I think of the surface of the river, the vast sky, the light breeze. I think of my salary of more than ten thousand riels. My electric lamp. I think of asphalt roads, running water, the radio, the television, all the beautiful songs we listen to. I remember everything.

NOTES

Excerpts from *The Accused* are taken from Khun Srun, *L'accusé*, trans. Christophe Macquet (Paris: Les Éditions du Sonneur, 2018). © Les Éditions du Sonneur, 2017.

1. Quoted in Hannah Arendt, *Men in Dark Times* (New York: Harcourt Brace, 1983), 165.

2. Taylor Owen and Ben Kiernan, "Bombs over Cambodia," *The Walrus*, October 2006, pp. 62–69.

3. Hannah Arendt, *Between Past and Future* (New York: Penguin, 2006), 87.

4. Ibid., 34.

5. This was the dream of many Cambodians, during the violent years of the civil war (1970–1975), prior to the Khmer Rouge genocide (1975–1979).

6. Khun Srun draws from Immanuel Kant who, in *Critique of Pure Reason*, writes that the questions "What can I know? What should I do? What may I hope?" together suggest the answer to the question "What is the human being?" Immanuel Kant, *Critique of Pure Reason*, trans. and ed. Paul Guyer and Allen W. Wood (Cambridge: Cambridge University Press, 1998), 677.

7. Krâm Ngoy was a well-known and beloved Cambodian bard during the time of the French protectorate. He died in 1936.

8. Herbert Marcuse was a Freudian-Marxist philosopher of the Frankfurt School. He was celebrated as a thinker by the European student movements of 1967–1968, and in Berlin, Rome, and Paris, the names of the "three M's" were written side-by-side on the walls. Marcuse died in 1979, at the age of eighty-one.

9. Jayavarman VII was one of the most influential and powerful rulers of the Khmer kingdom, renowned for his devotion to Buddhism. He reigned from 1181 to 1218.

10. French translator's note: The civil war is at present raging in Phnom Penh and throughout Cambodia.

11. Kakey is a tragic female figure in a classical and well-known Khmer fable.

12. Meursault is the French-Algerian hero of Albert Camus's *L'étranger*.

13. Saravan was a commandant of the Kampot region and received one of the first death sentences of the Khmer Republic under General Lon Nol. He was shot and killed in September 1970.

14. This refers to executions (often filmed) of opponents of Right and Left, at the end of the 1960s, when Norodom Sihanouk was removed from power and General Lon Nol installed in a military coup.

15. Khun Srun refers to Tum's murder in *Tum Teav*, a masterpiece of Cambodian poetry.

YELLOW FOR EPHEMERAL

Sam J. Miller

We were never meant to survive.
—Audre Lorde, "A Litany for Survival"

Yellow sun paints the pier boys, gilds the edges of their black and brown and pale pink skin. They lean against iron railings, do pull-ups on steel scaffolding. They smoke. They laugh. They make eyes at each other, at men or women passing by. Some are shirtless already. The day will be a hot one. It's the fifth one I've been alive. In two more, I'll be dead.

I don't know how I know this. I know lots of things and don't know how. There are also many things I don't know and don't know why not. First thing I remember is crawling, gasping, out of dense undergrowth, in a dark strip of forest at the western edge of a park. Wet with slime, coughing up thick brown fluid. Fully clothed, in the costume of a pier boy.

I sit on the bench. I've been sitting here since 3:00 A.M. I didn't sleep. I don't. I wandered the streets, laughed with strangers, broke up two fights, spoke easily and argued eloquently, made out with a pretty thing who had to hurry back before his last bus left Port Authority, all obeying instincts or programming I could not explain or trace. Then I came here. To watch the river, to watch the piers. Watch the boys. I look like one of them.

One of them thinks I *am* one of them.

"Hey," he says, sitting down. His wolf smile starts a warmth inside me. His bright yellow sleeveless shirt sets off the darkness of his shoulders. He has more stubble than me. "You've been here a while."

I shrug. It is an easy move, thoughtless. I smile, which is harder. A mere smile requires restraint. What I want to do is pounce on him. Ravish him.

"You hungry? I go to Holy Apostles, Thursdays. Pretty decent breakfast."

"Sounds good," I say, mouth watering for pancakes, which I have never tasted, eager even for the cheap sludge syrup they serve in soup kitchens. I follow him east, away from the water.

"Hop," he says, extending a hand.

"Crawford." It is my name.

"You're cute, Crawford."

"Look who's talking, Hop." And then I say his name again, several times, because I like saying it, and because he likes my saying it.

Machines on poles watch us go. Other machines buzz by overhead, scanning us, remembering us. Copying everything off of Hop's phone, in case it might be useful later. We are walking through a massive machine, built to watch us and wait for a chance to grab us.

Since crawling out of the mud, I've known: I must have a mission. There has got to be a reason I'm here. For five days I've been looking for it. Maybe Hop is taking me there.

Pancakes are as perfect as I imagined they'd be. The church is packed, and we sit at the edge where I can watch out the window. People fascinate me. I'm not the only thing in disguise. I see wolves in the shape of women, sweaty red-faced ghosts wearing the bodies of joggers. Some are stone. Some are wind. Few are as ephemeral as I am. Seven-year locust boys and the widows of Habsburg emperors head south on Ninth Avenue.

Newspaper headlines shriek in my direction. Walls going up; bombs going off. Morality militias. New laws about what can't be taught in school. Who can't learn what.

"Hey, Hop," says a man, easily ten years older than him, who frowns at me. "Protest, tonight. About the sex worker arrests. And the new deportations. You should come."

"Sure," Hop says, smiling, unaware of this poor creature's desperate love for him. A hookup, to Hop; nothing more.

"Sex worker arrests?" I ask, when he's gone.

"You know," Hop says. "Same old bullshit. Cops go after gay kids any way they can. Boy got roughed up a couple weeks ago, in custody, and it got a lot of attention. Situation's heating up."

"Yeah," I say, "same old bullshit," because this much is in my bones as well—all our natural predators, the ones who carry guns and the ones with knives for teeth, the ones behind pulpits and the ones whose suit coats hide twisting, coiled nests of venomous tentacles. "Good that something's happening about it."

"It's not something that's *happening*," he says. "It's something we're *doing*."

"Yes," I say, and his smile electrifies me, fills me up with possibilities, calls into question thousands of things I'd taken for granted as immutable. "Let's."

Back on the sidewalk, we drift.

"What kind of bug is that?" Hop asks, swatting at the air.

"Mayflies," I say, my voice hushed, reverent. "*Ephemeroptera*."

"Never seen them before. They seem to love you."

We buy lemon ices. Yellow gold drips from his chin. I want to lick it off, but I also want to watch it glisten there. Something tugs at me: the things I should be doing, the mission I should be finding and finishing. The sights I should be seeing. The things I've got to do, in the little time I have left to do them.

"Come on," I say, tonguing the drop and turning south.

"Where are we going?"

"Forward."

He laughs and follows. I scour every face we pass. I squat to pet dogs, peer into their eyes. Looking for it. Whatever it is. I open doors, step into bars and coffee shops and construction sites. Breathe in the smells. Every single one of them is exhilarating.

"You're contagious," he whispers.

"What do you mean?"

"How you see the city. Like you just got off the boat."

Like I'm seeing it all for the first time. And the last. Like in a couple of days I won't be able to see any of it, anymore.

"Like everything's amazing," he says, and his hand is hot and huge in the small of my back.

Everything's not amazing. The air is heavy with the stink of suffering. Fear, hunger, the crushing desperation of making rent. The faraway men working hard to make our lives miserable. Everywhere we go, police officers stare us down. Wondering what we are up to, whether we can help fill their weekly quota. I flinch away from all of them.

Will there be more, for me? After this? When I die, will I return? Another iteration of the same form, or some new shape—less ephemeral, perhaps, or less beautiful? Will it depend on what I do now, whether I accomplish whatever obscure action I'm here to realize? Will I remember any of this?

Gold is the most precious metal precisely because it is the weakest. The one that can't be used for armor or weapons, struts or steps or girders. It has no function beyond looking good. I think of that, watching Hop's back.

But diamonds are the most precious stones precisely because they are the strongest. Because they can't be broken; because only another diamond can cut one.

We drift slowly toward the protest. Soon the sound of shouting pulls us faster, its gravity inexorable, delirious. People are angry. People are excited. Police stand in a thin line, off to the side, and now it is they who are frightened of us.

We chant curses. We sing obscenities. The earth thumps with the rhythm of our feet.

And yes, I think, this *must* be it. I am standing at the center of the crowd, feeling their power surge through me, feeling mine in theirs; maybe this is what I'm here for, my mission, and I feel it all through me, my arms rise up almost on their own, and I howl.

Hop howls too. Claps me on the shoulder. Kisses me.

Nothing else happens. No fireball, no shattering of every glass window in the tall cold buildings looking down on us. But who is to say I haven't accomplished something, changed something, helped push a little harder against the silence? I catch a woman staring, and she smiles, and I know *she will remember that glimpsed howling boy for the rest of her life.*

We stagger off, after. Laugh with friends. Meet up at the piers. I can't let go of him. My body wants to melt into his. Mission, purpose, my impending dissolution—none of that matters. All I want is this. He takes my hand and leads me off the path and into a narrow strip of dense woodland beside the river.

In the undergrowth, we fuck like animals. Hop's weight is on top of me; my arms are around a tree trunk. Rough bark presses against my bare stomach; yellow lichens wrinkle my nose; I am a boy-shaped bubble of bliss, and as he drags me toward orgasm, I am certain I'll pop like a balloon.

All that happens is I inseminate the soil at the foot of the tree.

We get coffee, after. We are twitchy, touchy, electrified.

"I got to go see my mom," he says. "Out in Far Rockaway. I'd ask you to come, only she doesn't . . ."

"Like to be reminded," I say, reading the specific shame on his face.

"No."

"It's okay," I say. "I understand."

"She's having some health issues. I'll need to be there a day or two."

"Of course."

Hop's face looks hopeful, frightened. "Maybe you could give me your number?"

"Phone got stolen," I said. "Haven't been able to scrape together enough for a new one." I take his hand, hold it. It's a stupid move, dangerous, not what cool pier boys do, but it makes him smile. Which makes me. "I'll be here," I say.

I secretly follow him down from the street, hide behind a column on the platform, ride the train to Far Rockaway in the next car. Watch him through the window in the door. He looks sad, or exhausted. Probably both. He stares into his phone; he calls someone. He dozes, most of the way. His legs twitch in his sleep.

Probably he is telling the truth. Probably he wants to see me again. Probably I am not a one-day fling, the single slice of romance that will satisfy his hunger for it for another month or year. But if I am, I'm not certain this upsets me.

It's dawn when the train arrives at the end of the line. He gets off, blinking in the little light. I can smell the sea. He walks in that direction. I watch him go. He is very small and getting smaller. A yellow, ephemeral shred. Then I get back on the train and wait for it to take me back.

Full daylight by the time I get back to the trees beside the river. The same yellow mushrooms litter the floor of the clearing—but something new is here now. Precisely where my semen splattered the earth is a huge ochre growth, tumored with lumps and thick fissures. Like the biggest mushroom you ever saw, big enough to house an adult human in the fetal position, but it is no mushroom. I know this. I squat down, and I can smell it, the thing inside, the heavy male reek of it. I press my ear against the membrane and hear the weak rapid thumping of its heart.

This can't have been my purpose. There must be more to me than making my replacement.

I want to kick it open, tear the fetal me inside to pieces. Punish it for presuming to take my place, breathe my air, stand in the sun when I cannot. But that won't give me a single extra second of life. My clock started ticking the second I tore my way out of my own placental fungus. I rub the sticky surface of the mushroom. Feel its heat. Wish it well. Whatever I am, its powers are limited and its purpose unclear, and survival was never an option.

THE RETINUE OF LITTLE ABYSSES

Juan Martinez

1

The abyss tips his red hat, says nothing.
Says, I've got all this nothing for you.

2

The abyss insists it is not an abyss,
insists on coming over for dinner,
says he's hurt—why didn't you invite him in?
He's here, at any rate. He brought a dish,
a mesh bag with two live rabbits,
your neighbor's pets.

I'm here, he says. Let's eat.

3

The abyss writes his inaugural address
on the back of the middle-school journal
he dug from the yard
of your childhood home.

He cribs the part where you called
your crush the absolute worst.

Also the part where you wished your parents dead
Also the part where you mourned your mom.

The abyss draws a heart where you drew a heart.

He wipes the dirt from the cover,
smears blood on the spine,
your papercut, now his.
This, he says, is mine.

The abyss writes in his name
buries yours.

4

The abyss left eleven voicemails
on the night of his party
to say, You're not invited,
to say, Why aren't you here?
Everyone's here, everyone
who didn't want to be here
is here, he says. But the room
echoes. No one's there.
The abyss says he didn't want
this party. That he threw it for you.
That you're already there
in the empty room. The abyss
says he'll never call again
right before he calls again
to say he's done calling.

5

The abyss builds a wall
around nothing, another around
his empty stomach. He builds
another wall around the first
to keep the builders in:

Your cousins, their hands
raw from building
walls that keep nothing in.

Wind sweeps into the abyss.
So do birds. So do bricks.

The abyss eats the wall
you build. The abyss
looks at your red hands,
your raw face.
It's fine, he says,
We'll build again.

6

The abyss broke your microwave
to find a bug that wasn't there,
the same bug your mother used
to listen in on every secret she wanted
kept from her: Your cruelty to friends,
small animals. Every birthday you forgot.
Every call of hers you ignored,
every lie you told, every excuse
you made that could not be believed
that she believed.

The abyss believes
this bug—bottle green, abuzz,
every wire alive with your lies.
The abyss calls your mom
to let her know.

Your mom cries,
hangs up, calls back. The bug
responds. Records. The abyss
listens in. Says, You know.
You've always known.
You tapped my wires.
You know.

                      Your mom sighs,
nods. You listen in. You try
not to. The abyss does
not hang up.

7

The abyss lets go
of his own arms, of the sour air
that fills his invisible limbs.

His eyes, too—never useful,
now free, and not his own.
Never his, he tells you,
each eye a Mylar balloon

lost by a child at a state fair.
Yours, the abyss says.
Your child. Or your balloon.

The abyss lets go
of every part of him
but his mouth
and that is all the sky is
every day, every night:
the mouth of the abyss.

8

The abyss asks that you please not laugh.
His retinue says the same. The retinue

of little abysses demands respect, silence,
a smidgen of fear. Won't you please fear him,

please? Won't you shake at the immensity
of his nothingness? Won't you cry or rage

or at the very least call back? We're lonely
here with the abyss, say the little abysses.

We have nothing, can say nothing. Don't
laugh, and we'll disclose everything

we learned, every thought and secret act:
the small sin, the vast lie. You'll laugh.

Listen: We heard his every waking word,
and—no joke—what we learned is nothing.

RECLAIMING TIME

Airea D. Matthews

3:00 A.M.

night's shroud will cover you
sure as morning. turning
on the bed you've craved,
awake with headlines still breaking.
in the faint distance, a ghost train barrels
northwest, carrying whatever it carries.
no day has ever bared any tracks, yet
you know they're there by the rhythm
of the unrelenting wheel blade. trains,
spirits, and white noise are familiars at this
hour, and two of them you routinely ignore
while shuffling to a chilled corner
to write what matters to only very few:
this world will unlikely end// (tomorrow, but it may)
it's ill and always has been// (as far as memory serves)
though memory is no servant.

3:15 A.M.

SERVICE   the period before
bodies

              return to senders
                    if found

3:30 A.M.

POWER   an ailment
        cockspur burrowing into clay

4:00 A.M.

when the sun rises, will the sickness value
your sons above a sweat bead, field, or ring?

which patriotic carpetbagger will thirst
for your daughters the way they thirst
for their own? who will do something
about silent blue walls
& the black tax & electricity
& missiles & glacial shifts
& Internet crypts & collusion
& the enemy & hero myths
& new neuroses & CNN
& press briefings & safe haven
& tweets
& the witless
& the cunning & questions to which
you already know the answers?

5:00 A.M.

DIVISION is math   is a war strategy—
attack the flank

5:15 A.M.

ALTERNATIVE FACT   safety is . . .   is myth
          is the head of a match   is a fingernail tip

6:00 A.M.

of course, you could expel those
ruminations. consider the wind,
for God's sake! it's rapping panes as
a rattler approaches. it's beautiful, right?
everything's fucking perfect
those few seconds before
sleep's organ of flight
fills the lull
and you might believe, really believe,
these times demand nothing from
dreaming men before they wake.

6:15 A.M.

COVFEFE   partridges fly in coveys   are light sleepers
lucid   slow waves
less vulnerable to predators   ready

6:30 A.M.

your father's fathers
your mother's mothers
took wing in deep slumber,
mid-dream of picket fences,
awaiting copper promises.

6:45 A.M.

WALL is a feeble hedge   is side effect
                the drowning yew, trench-
        planted

7:00 A.M.

your body rises
despite gravity's
forceful jostling.
budding sun defies
moon's malaise.
and you, resistant
to night's inconstant
pinion and roveries
meant to daunt,
know dark hours
bury no truths
light won't unroot.

To Our Americas

YEAR OF THE RAT

Marc Anthony Richardson

Prison is a better place, the television tells me, for on State Road, a warren
of weigh stations of jails not a prison, the second son was less prosperous.
Since Illuminati has replaced me I am free to take the mother's place for
virtual visitation, for her left knee is oppressive; I have taken a regional train
from outside the city to the center of the city to walk toward the Society,
addled by muscatel, to hear the television promote more freedom in prison,
more privileges, only two to a room, more options and better classes, plenty
of time to study and genuflect without the fret of debt. I listen to it intently,
because sometimes I fantasize: maybe I'll learn to be a good little conduit,
maybe I'll create some unexampled masterpiece by pulling a rabbit out
of my ass and having it luxuriate in tertiary tones, or maybe I'll just burn
a book into their souls instead—maybe I'll feel about my words the way
Baldwin felt about his: *I love writing so much that when I die I want to die
in the middle of a sentence.* Yes, maybe I'll just crawl on out of my foxhole
because I'm tired of staying free. If I cannot satisfy the wanderlust, if I
cannot make my way toward the solitudes *to lurk in crystalline thought like
the trout under verdurous banks, where stray mankind should only see my
bubble come to the surface,*[1] then I shall stroll straight in there and mark my
fear off the calendar—for like a stray, sooner or later, after a godless fuck,
I'm going to get hit. I'm going to get up and go right out into traffic and get
run-ed-ed over really nice and good.

But State Road is an intermediate state where little or no privileges
are to be had or gained, where you and all of the other complaints are
packed into an overcrowded holding cell to feed off of each another,
where you storm into a compound of storms: the manifold glut of gripes
from sodomites and rapists and butchers and reapers and soft-spoken
peacekeepers, who are all sexually attracted to children, *short eyes*, all
lumped together in there like one big stool, all complaining and sneezing
and snoring and hawking and spitting and shouting and shitting and—
oh, god, the fury of cocks; only to be shifted from one holding cell to
another, and then another and another until you are finally thankful to
be integrated into a large wing where a plastic spork could peek up from
a breast pocket like a pet (for after dedicating myself to the arts I've been
encaged several times, twice in there although only for a few weeks; yet

during those times I learned that you can *never* lose your spork, because eating oatmeal with your ass-wiping hand maybe downright degrading, but you damn sure would do it). State Road: a strip of correctional facilities belying their efficacies in the northeast quadrant of this city (one of which being the wheel-and-spoke designed and designated House of Corrections), where some of its detention units accommodate close to two hundred and fifty men on two tiers inside eight sizeable cells, four on either side of this immense warehouse of a wing divided by an open space shaped like a diamond with a guard station in the middle, with only two shower stalls and three commodes to relieve the thirty or so men in their given accommodation. No one's supposed to be in there for long, though, a year at most, and once you're convicted you're transported to and processed at SCI Graterford, just west of the city, a seventeen-hundred-and-thirty-acre thirty-foot-high-walled nine-towered (manned by sharpshooters) double-gated airlocked shiny bright hell, stomaching over thirty-five hundred souls, a penal farm where various factories generate a revenue of millions while paying the prisoners peanuts, a place where a prisoner of conscience, a journalist with dreadlocks, has been paddling down the eddies of death row for over twenty-five years, and where you are asked upon arrival: Where would you like your body sent? After Graterford the second son was transported to SCI Camp Hill (not far from the firstborn) and then finally over to the newly mushroomed SCI Pine Grove, to a small county on the far western side of this state (the Christmas Tree Capital of the World, Ku Klux Klan territory) in a grand-scale effort to upscale states by providing dependable revenue, to a maximum-security prison where at thirty-two and a model inmate he could mentor youths adjudicated as adults; but before his conviction, inside a swarming cell, State Road held him for *two* years as the judicial juggernaut deliberated postponed stalled and forgot about a lot, only to give him a minimum of ten and a maximum of twenty (this being his third small-time infraction within the span of fifteen years)—yet all that judge had to do was *sneeze* and the evidence would've been gone.

On State Road I've seen men beaten by women so badly, he says, that their own women would walk right pass them in the visiting room. Once when I was en route to this open-spaced visiting room he's referring to, this female guard—most of the guards are uneducated blacks—had a mother removed from line and placed inside a small room for her to undo the child's diaper and then for her to strip herself: a regulation and yet at one's discretion, for the guard had just let another mother pass through without any provocation; and inside that air-conditioned nightmare the guard had fixed the woman's son with such presumptive disdain that, later in the lobby, she told me that the guard had been beaten barren, that she had shared the same room with her in the same sorority. Of course, at their discretion, two male guards with latex gloves and aplomb would take me into a room, while the second son would be taken into another: Take off your clothes, they would say to us, open your mouth lift your tongue bend spread them and cough—which felt oddly analogous to when we were being beaten as boys. Sometimes the male guard executing the directive was a latent homosexual, for one guard had to lay down his post outside the visiting room because he couldn't cope with the nightmares: people popping up in places where they oughtn't be popping up. A known homosexual was asked to search the second son once, and although his hair was often braided by men, men who love men, he was so emasculated that he would've never had the visit had not the visitor been his mother, a link to the outside, whom by another's discretion had been asked to lift up her breasts drop her pants bend spread them and cough. So that when they entered the visiting room, like the currency and the take-out carton revolved inside the tiny two booths, the prisoner and the visitor were exchanged.

The female guards, boomeranging from abuses, coagulating from rapes, can be of the most vindictive stock—as well as the most opportunistic: On State Road I could've had a woman any time I wanted, the second son admits, and in this virtual visitation room the screen is so revolutionarily clear that I can almost reach in to touch the braids of this television evangelist. There is no plexiglass encasement; nor is the camera composing my eye, perched atop his television, protected: provocation from an ill-received virtual visit would be unbridled, which makes me feel as though I am talking to a test subject in orange coveralls, contrasted by the white room and sitting upright at an unbolted-down metal table and chair to prove that the product's no further a threat. And yet not fully so. Rubbernecking is pretty common on State Road, he says; the female guards look into your books to see how much money you have, and if you have a roll, they would proposition you: Just last week, here at Pine Grove, I'm sitting here in the cell, right, when this woman comes in and stands right next to me and says, So what you are drawing?—mind you, a guard can *never* be alone in a cell with an inmate. (Just then, behind him, I see a face in the window on the door before it disappears.) I'm scared stiff, he says, back against the wall, sweating; I have a few hundred on my books from drawing commissions and working men's cases, so when she comes into my cell and starts asking questions and touching my arm, like this, I have to remind her of who I really am and what I really do—give Sunday services and everything. She gives me a look then and smiles as though she's sorry—mind you, this is the same woman who had another guard stomp a man into wine on steel stairs for saying something foul to her: she was servicing them both. And that man, the case I was working, still recovering from a shooting, had his colostomy bag burst. She even had me stomped for trying to stop it, and then thrown into the hole; *Mount Sinai* we call it— and here *she* is with the ovaries to ask me to pray over her . . . privately. . . . I guess you can't look down on someone you look up to, because she takes the storage keys and takes me up there, and it seems like she's sincere, you know, but I'm afraid of a trap: I haven't made love in so long. Yet it had just rained, and I was watching the sun coming through the mesh fortifying the windows, like a web drenched in dew, lit up by the light, and I was wondering about that alabaster box of ointment, about how that prostitute had anointed the Master's feet with her own tears and then dried them with her hair, about how the Pharisee had scowled at her act of love and what the Master had said: He who is forgiven much has much to love—and about whom *she* must have to forgive, if only for herself. *Forgiveness is the fragrance*, she said, *that the violet sheds on the heel that has crushed it.*[2]

He asks why I'm asking about this, and I have to remind him of who I am, of the upcoming court hearing and there can be no more postponements: Yes yes, he says, you always had to be a little hungry. But whatever you do, though, don't go in there like a guilty man. Hear me now: what is falling apart could be coming together, so I will keep the best of you, little brother, until you can keep it for yourself, a keepsake. And my eyes my eyes . . . I don't restrain it. After a moment I wipe them and ask him how he's been, has the firstborn visited him? He has. He talked about having gone into our house, about our father's apartment: He should have never died the way he did, he said, half-exposed. I apologize to the second son for not having gone out there this summer, for not having his daughter here today: she was seven when he went in; she'll be seventeen soon. I don't think he would even be in there if it wasn't for that officer, the one who threw him down the stairs while hall-sweeping in high school for illegalities; I ask him if he remembers the father—the one person who we thought would defend his son's innocence—taking the officer's side, and he says that even *with* that concussion he remembers . . . but don't be too hard on him: How many of us could have said we were tired of going to Disney World? And now look at us, I say. One of the *sons of Ham* will be laughing in the Oval Office. The window face returns and taps the door for him to turn nod and return to me. I used to fight for my time away from you, he says. Now I wish we had more sand together. I say it's been running through our fingers ever since we took our plates to our television sets. Now look at us, he says. The only time we see each other is through a screen.

Notes

This piece is excerpted from Marc Anthony Richardson, *Year of the Rat* (Tuscaloosa: University of Alabama Press, 2016). Reprinted with permission of University of Alabama Press.

1. Richardson references Thoreau here. See Henry David Thoreau, *The Journal of Henry David Thoreau*, vol. 3 (Layton, UT: Peregrine Smith Books, 1984), 133.

2. Here Richardson references a quotation often attributed to Mark Twain, who is said to have been quoting an asylum inmate.

BULLET POINTS

Jericho Brown

I will not shoot myself
In the head, and I will not shoot myself
In the back, and I will not hang myself
With a trash bag, and if I do,
I promise you, I will not do it
In a police car while handcuffed
Or in the jail cell of a town
I only know the name of
Because I have to drive through it
To get home. Yes, I may be at risk,
But I promise you, I trust the maggots
Who live beneath the floorboards
Of my house to do what they must
To any carcass more than I trust
An officer of the law of the land
To shut my eyes like a man
Of God might, or to cover me with a sheet
So clean my mother could have used it
To tuck me in. When I kill me, I will kill me
The same way most Americans do,
I promise you: cigarette smoke
Or a piece of meat on which I choke
Or so broke I freeze
In one of these winters we keep
Calling worst. I promise that if you hear
Of me dead anywhere near
A cop, then that cop killed me. He took
Me from us and left my body, which is,
No matter what we've been taught,
Greater than the settlement a city can
Pay a mother to stop crying, and more
Beautiful than the brand new bullet
Fished from the folds of my brain.

DOMESTIC TERRORISM

Cynthia Atkins

I'll tell you about terrorism—the suicide bomber in your car, strapped and loaded and tendered next to you, breathing hard—the bad breath of God. Cartoon-blue Fourth of July sky, until a thunderclap hurls everything into an illness. The father is a panic of heat, mad as gasoline. The mother's lips wilt into lettuce and then munitions. Endless cars out the window gaslight your imaginings. Speedometer jacking from 50 to 95 mph. Now their words are cocking in rounds—blood sputters on the porridge of the book in your lap. You want to touch the ears of all the commas on the page. You want "Goldilocks" to take you into this village of thatched roofs and innocence. It is the Fourth of July. America is the space between their brutal mouths. You dangle like a thimble in this giant's wicked hands. Terror smacks you in this grid of panic and doom, cornered crude windowed jail.

I'll tell you about terror, the kind you feel when the neighborhood boys are chasing you home to see what's under your skirt, the downy fur between your legs. They want to own it. Terror is your voice going mute over every sidewalk and city block. Your throat tied and gagged at the bottom of a river. The parents now have bubbles of silence coming out of their mouths. Terror is the heat impaling us all. At home, you know the dog is burling out of her fur. She's under the bed trying not to wet the rug, when *the bad boys* set off their wares in the dark, between the wide thighs of the sky. Terror. You're trying not to pee on the vinyl in the back seat. You want to swap places with Goldilocks sleeping in her safe, borrowed bed. You want to climb in this book, tip over a rustic chair to prove you were there.

I'll show you terror when God is a bluesman on the radio, blowing in the crosshairs between the cars—all this rage and debris. Your father, a salesman unloved by this woman next to him. Your mother would tootle at the beauty shop, while your father took lithium. A body could explode with this grief. Your heart is a flag at half-mast. Terror is the time your boss took you to his scuzzy back seat, became the intruder in your own house of solitude. *What sharp hands he had.* Every action has a terrible twin. Your blue dress flew out the window. A blue dot on the highway. Every dictator knows there is power in fear. There is darkness. The dog presses under the bed, wetting the rug. *The bad boys* blast firecrackers between your legs. Terror is not bliss—it is invisible and dangerous. It brings hearts home in body bags. It gags your mouth with stones.

THE LEGEND OF *BIG* AND *FINE*

Jericho Brown

Long ago, we used two words
For the worth of a house, a car,
A woman—all the same to men
Who claimed them: things
To be entered, each to suffer
Wear and tear with time, but
Greater than the love for these
Was the strong little grin
One man offered another
Saying, *You lucky. You got you*
A big, fine _____.
Hard to imagine so many men
Waiting on each other to be
Recognized, every crooked
Tooth in our naming mouths
Ready like the syllables
Of a very short sentence, each
Crying *mine*, like infants who
Grab for what must be beautiful
Since someone else saw it.

WHO HAS THE RIGHT TO TELL THIS STORY?

HOW ART AND ARTISTS CAN HELP AND HARM PEOPLE EXPERIENCING ADDICTION

Liz Moore

The Kensington neighborhood is the center of opioid abuse in Philadelphia, which itself is one of the centers of opioid abuse on the East Coast. There were nine hundred opioid overdoses in the city in 2016, according to the Philadelphia Department of Public Health.[1] In 2009, the year I first went to Kensington with the photographer Jeffrey Stockbridge, there were fewer than half that many. The problem, in other words, is escalating each year, with no signs of stopping.

One cannot walk up Kensington Avenue without seeing multiple women seeking clients for sex work to fund the purchase of opioids, or multiple people in various states of opioid intoxication. One cannot pass through nearby parks and empty lots without seeing discarded syringes, baggies, and other paraphernalia. The *Philadelphia Inquirer* once referred to a particular part of Kensington as a "hellscape," a term that some deem problematic.[2] Nevertheless, it is clear upon visiting Kensington that many of its residents are experiencing pain and suffering in a variety of ways.

For the past year, I've been working on a novel set partially in Kensington that includes characters who are experiencing addiction and characters who are affected by it. The process of writing it has caused me to question the role of artists who wish to portray addiction, even those of us who have some personal connection to it.

The urge to explore addiction artistically makes sense: artists have always been drawn to highly fraught emotional territory, and what is art if not an exploration of humanity in all of its facets—including human suffering? And yet there exists a clear ethical obligation to engage with members of a particular population rather than exploiting them, to elevate the voice of a population rather than elevating one's own artistic voice above one's subjects.

In this essay, I explore my own draw to writing about addiction, and I explore the work of photographer Jeffrey Stockbridge, with whom I've collaborated in the past. I also include conversations I've had with two people in various stages of recovery—both of whom Jeff has photographed—and with several people who work in the field of addiction treatment and/or community activism through art. In writing this essay, I hope to clarify for myself some of the moral obligations I have as a writer exploring an issue that causes real trauma in many people's daily lives.

Questions and Concerns

People who have experienced addiction—both those with active addiction and those in recovery—can be in emotionally fragile states. And it can be difficult to discern an active user's level of intoxication in a given moment. Both issues raise questions about whether the subject of a photograph, an interview, or any other artistic intervention is well equipped to give consent.

Another question that applies, even when consent is given, is under what circumstances art that centers on addiction is exploitative. And a third is how this art affects public perception of addiction and those who experience it.

In the midst of a year of national turmoil following the election of Donald Trump, when many different demographic groups are experiencing a profound sense of isolation and, in some cases, a concern for their physical and mental safety, there is real urgency to the idea of looking out for the needs of one's neighbors. In my case, and in the case of everyone else making art that centers on addiction, I believe it is incumbent on us to ensure that the subjects of our art are neither exploited nor harmed by it.

My Work

I never talk about my work in progress; I'm superstitious about it. But I've been working on my fourth novel for about a year now, and for the first time I feel it's important to talk about it as I work, to engage with the people whose lives mirror those of my characters, and to make sure, above all, that I'm being respectful of their experience. That I'm getting it as right as I can.

So here it is: The subject of the novel I'm writing is addiction. More specifically, opioid addiction. Even more specifically, opioid addiction in Kensington, Philadelphia. The main characters are siblings, one of whom is in the throes of this addiction, the other of whom is experiencing the intense daily anxiety caused by having a loved one who continuously falls into and out of sobriety.

This is not the first time I've written about addiction; in my second novel, *Heft*, one character is addicted to alcohol, and another deals with compulsive eating. But it's the first time I've written about opioid addiction and the first time I've written about a topic that is so much in the news.

If "What are you writing?" is the most difficult question to answer, then "Why are you writing it?" is the second. The first answer to that question is that there is a long history of addiction in my family, generations of it. There is also a long history of recovery—both sustained and intermittent but generally successful enough that I did not personally experience the trauma that many addiction-adjacent children do. I can't get into specifics because they're not my specifics to get into. But I can say two things:

1. Because of my family's history, I spent a lot of time thinking about and talking about addiction as a kid, and I often sought out books, films, and television shows that dealt with it.
2. The addiction that members of my family have experienced was and is, as far as I know, not to opioids.

The second answer is that one of my first experiences in Philadelphia, when I moved here in 2009, involved collaborating with Jeff as he made portraits of and interviewed the subjects of his series *Kensington Blues.* That series, which began with portraits of women engaged in sex work to fund their addiction to heroin and opioids but eventually expanded to include a variety of Kensington's residents and some of its scenery, cemented itself in my brain.

Since 2009, opioid abuse in Philadelphia and around the country has grown into a serious concern; words like *crisis* and *epidemic* daily find their way into newspaper headlines, and Kensington has been used nationally and internationally as an illustration of the problem. But when Jeff began visiting, the media had only begun to pick up on the issue, and I didn't know what to expect before my first visit there.

Jeff's Work

Jeff has, since that time, amassed a huge amount of material for *Kensington Blues*, much of which can be viewed on his blog of the same title. Notably, many of the posts on this blog include audio recordings in which his subjects tell their own stories. Some also include photographs of handwritten notes that Jeff's subjects write as he photographs them. For example, one couple wrote the following notes:

> One part, one piece of the never ending circle of life. Life as at least I know it. Life as you can see it, the hardships, the loneliness, the hopelessness, pretty much the walking dead. Kensington is one of a kind. The people are unlike any other in any place in the world. It's an ironic uniqueness, ironic because it's unique in the sense that

Krista, January 2011. (Photograph by Jeffrey Stockbridge.)

it's set apart because of the drugs, prostitution, + street soldiers. I'm one piece of the puzzle + hope that like Jeff I too can show the true identity of real life as we know it. —Carissa

Kensington is not just drugs and violence and prostitution. There are people here who live and love life. Behind all the negative issues, there is a community that strives to live here and will not leave. It's all that they know. I have a beautiful girl that loves me as much as I love her. And together we can do anything. What the media portrays North Philly and Kensington as isn't true. There are those of us who are trying to do right and live life. I am happy despite the situation I'm in. And I will continue to be happy. —M.Z.[3]

Jeff's work wasn't initially meant to include addiction. In fact, he says, he didn't realize the women he was shooting were addicted. "I began with photographing women who were standing on corners, showing them pictures, saying, 'What do you know about the neighborhood? Tell me about the neighborhood.' Asking them to share their wisdom."[4] But soon addiction became the subject.

Jeff wasn't the first photographer, of course, to be drawn to those experiencing addiction. In 1964 and 1965, the writer James Mills and the photographer Bill Eppridge spent two months documenting the lives of a couple addicted to heroin. The resulting *Time* magazine photo-essay, "John and Karen, Two Lives Lost to Heroin"—which also served as the inspiration for the 1971 film *The Panic in Needle Park*—was the first of many photo-essays to portray addiction for a popular audience. Subsequent photographic series include Larry Clark's controversial 1971 *Tulsa* and his 1983 series *Teenage Lust* and John Ranard's *The Fire Within*, which documents drug use in Russia.

Each of these examples has sometimes been described as documentary in nature. The implication of the phrase *documentary photography* is that the artist plays a neutral role, simply capturing life as it is. In an essay on the work of Ranard in the *International Journal of Drug Policy*, scholar John L. Fitzgerald suggests that documentary photography is rather a kind of sleight of hand. "Put simply, photographs are made rather than taken. There is more to drug photography than just being a mirror to the world. Documentary photography however continues to cite its objectivity and more than any other filmic form 'produces nature as a guarantee of its truth.'"[5]

Because of the inclusion of first-person writing and audio clips, Jeff's work is different from other photography that centers on drug use and addiction; his project offers a model for an artist intervening in the lives of people in crisis. He provides his subjects with a platform from which to speak for themselves, rather than remaining passive subjects of another person's work. Also, in creating a blog, Jeff has—intentionally or unintentionally—created a forum for the Kensington community to connect and react to some of the issues it's presently facing.

Krista, January 2014. (Photograph by Jeffrey Stockbridge.)

As a forum, *Kensington Blues* appears to have therapeutic value, at least according to a few of the clients. Typical comments left on the blog are often deeply personal—sometimes critical, often compassionate. Many express hope for a subject's recovery or encourage those who have recently gotten into recovery. Under a follow-up post about one of Jeff's subjects who had found her way into recovery, one commenter—presumably a friend of the subject's—wrote:

God Bless you, Krista. Thank you for taking care of yourself. I'm
really happy to see you're doing good these days.

Another wrote:

I have been following all the stories on here for many years now, Im
so very happy you got out, I know what a hard battle that is to do,
and it just makes me so happy that your story turned out good. My
sister died on the streets of Camden from a heroin overdose, she
would get clean then go back, over and over again till she lost the
battle. Like I said, I'm extremely happy that you got out and got
your life back. Best of luck to you!

The subject herself wrote in the comments:

Hey. Krista here. Thanx for all the great comments and support.
Reading those comments brought tears to my eyes. Thanx to Jeff
for interviewing me again. It's so weird to see my old self knowing
who I am now, but I'm grateful for the opportunity and hopefully
someone else will read this and know that they don't have to keep
living that way. Never forget. But move on.[6]

Art as Therapy and More

A therapist at a nearby inpatient rehab facility, who asked to be identified
as Clarence, says that art therapy (notably different from Jeff's project) can
be essential to recovery. The art therapist uses art therapy to "to tap into
something that the client might not be willing to disclose about their past,
tapping into childhood issues, other issues that may have led to their self-
medication. Because that's really what we're dealing with a lot of the time—
greater, deeper psychiatric issues."[7] University of Pennsylvania addiction
specialist Charles O'Brien, who runs a treatment center, says, "I would be
in favor of it if it's in combination with medication, but if it's art by itself, it
will fail."[8]

The hope for art therapy has been extended in Kensington to the entire
community through a program called Kensington Storefront, in which
anyone—people with addiction, their family members, and sober people—
can work with a behavioral health specialist or an artist in a communal and
mutually supportive environment. The program is a collaboration between
the private nonprofit Porch Light and the city's Mural Arts Program and
Department of Behavioral Health. There I met Signe Espinoza, a staff
member of the Mural Arts Program who is running the storefront. Signe

was born in Kensington and moved back to the neighborhood as an adult. She now serves the neighborhood as a community activist and political organizer. Signe says that she has to make sure artists understand their role. "What I know is that I have a plan for artists who maybe aren't from this neighborhood to engage with the community," she says, "and be respectful of the community, because you're not here to educate them, you're not here to exploit them, you're not here to question them. You're here to offer some kind of service—service through art, service through concrete services."[9]

But in a nontherapeutic context, can art, and artists, help mitigate the crisis? Zoe Van Orsdol, community development associate at Impact Services, a job training and support agency in Kensington, says that art can be a gateway to treatment and healing. "Art brings people in," she says, describing a mural project called the Community Impact Lab that engages community members and veterans. "You think, okay, art, sure, that's great, but it's a sign to the neighborhood that things are changing, that change is possible. Somebody has taken an interest other than them, [and they] often feel like they work in isolation to try to improve the neighborhood."[10]

Jeff didn't set out to help people. While he has donated substantially to organizations that work with addicted people in Kensington, his photography, he says, is a "selfish pursuit." At the same time, *Kensington Blues* contributes to Van Orsdol's model of healing by countering the objectification of people with addiction. "What it does," he says, "is it challenges our preconceived notion of who is a heroin addict. First and foremost, they are a human being."[11]

Artistic Subjects Speak for Themselves

With that ideal in mind, I recently contacted two people who self-identify as being in recovery from addiction who were subjects of Jeff's photography. I wanted to get their perspectives on how art and artists can serve those with addiction and also to ask them whether art about addiction ever feels exploitative.

The first person I spoke with, Matt N., was photographed by Jeff on at least two separate occasions while he was actively using heroin and other narcotics. Matt, who was chronically homeless, is now in medication-assisted recovery and—through the help of Philadelphia-based organizations Prevention Point, Project HOME, and the Journey of Hope Project—has found permanent housing. Matt says that working with Jeff helped him discover a sense of community. "I think I was more interested in the fact of just being a part of something else. . . . I guess I had run into him a couple of other times that I remember, because I do remember looking through different photos that he had, and a lot of it was a sense

Matt, February 2012. (Photograph by Jeffrey Stockbridge.)

of reconnecting with people that had been photographed before, too, memories of them."[12]

I then asked Matt if he could see any downside to being photographed, and he said, "Not that I can think of." He elaborated:

> I think it's a good idea just because—I don't know—artists have a similar energy. Nonthreatening. They can relate a lot to what's

going on on the ground level. It's a way for [people] to take a break, to seek respite from their day.[13]

After Matt, I met with and interviewed Jerry (not his real name), another one of Jeff's subjects. Jerry has been in and out of recovery for prescription opioid medication for decades. He lost a stepdaughter to a heroin overdose and a brother, who suffered at length from addiction himself, to suicide. Jeff photographed Jerry, who was working as an outreach volunteer in Kensington, as he gave a shot of opiate antidote Narcan to someone overdosing on heroin (or, more likely, fentanyl). Jerry now makes a point to carry Narcan on him at all times.

I was curious to talk to Jerry because, unlike most of Jeff's other subjects, he had not initially given his consent to be photographed, though he did later.

Matt, January 2017. (Photograph by Jeffrey Stockbridge.)

I asked Jerry about his thoughts on Jeff's work and more generally about the influx of media and artistic attention in Kensington. "Is it helpful, harmful, or both?" I asked. Jerry responded:

> You know what? I don't think it makes a difference. Because they didn't go down there and start living under the bridge and shooting up heroin to get their picture in the paper. And to be honest with you, they could care less if they get their picture taken, because they're at a point now where they don't care. And it's really sad to see it. . . . Your heart goes out to them, because they're human beings. They're somebody's son, somebody's mother, or daughter, or sister, or brother. It's just tough to see, you know.[14]

Other subjects of Jeff's work, upon entering recovery, have occasionally contacted him to make a follow-up portrait. Although I didn't speak with them personally, Jeff has posted audio clips of his interviews with them, along with written transcripts of these interviews. Krista, mentioned previously, described her emotions while viewing herself in Jeff's work. "I'm kinda fascinated by looking at pictures of myself when, you know, I was using," she says. "I'd like to keep them as a reminder because I know myself—that I'd get high one time and I'd be right back, standing out there."[15]

Conclusion

Both Jeffrey Stockbridge and I entered Kensington as outsiders and were inspired to make art in different forms. Both of us have grappled (and still grapple) with what our responsibilities are as artists coming in from outside. Jeff, unlike me, has spent countless hours there over the past decade; he is now a known face in Kensington, has friends there, and rents a studio nearby. He is donating a portion of the sales from the art book he published, also called *Kensington Blues*, to Prevention Point, a not-for-profit organization that specializes in harm-reduction efforts in the neighborhood. Jeff has paid his dues in a way that I clearly haven't yet.

This is where I am as I continue my work on my novel: curious about what I can do to serve the community I'm writing about, hopeful that I can continue to engage with organizations like the Kensington Storefront and Prevention Point and with individuals who have been affected by addiction, and hopeful that the finished novel will not cause harm to the community in which it's set. Recently, I have begun to lead writing workshops at the Thea Bowman Women's Center, a day shelter in Kensington that serves a population with similarities to the characters I'm writing about in my novel. My intention is certainly to contribute positively to the neighborhood, but intentions are different from results.

I'm also aware, as I write my novel and as I write this piece, that I'm biased; I *want* to find absolution and approval for my work, and I want to feel as if I'm on the right side of something important. Whether I am is, ultimately, up to the community to decide—not me.

NOTES

1. Philadelphia Department of Public Health, "2016 Overdoses from Opioids in Philadelphia," *Chart* 2, no. 7 (2017): 1–3, available at https://www.phila.gov/health/pdfs/chart%20v2e7.pdf.

2. Sam Wood and Stephanie Farr, "Philly and Conrail to Clean Up 'Heroin Hellscape,'" *Philadelphia Inquirer*, June 15, 2017, available at http://www.philly.com/philly/health/addiction/city-and-conrail-reach-deal-to-address-heroin-hellscape-20170615.html.

3. Jeffrey Stockbridge, "Matt and Carissa," *Kensington Blues*, April 30, 2015, available at https://kensingtonblues.com/2015/04/30/matt-and-carissa.

4. Jeffrey Stockbridge, personal communication, August 10, 2017.

5. John L. Fitzgerald, "Drug Photography and Harm Reduction: Reading John Ranard," *International Journal of Drug Policy* 13, no. 5 (2002): 370.

6. Jeffrey Stockbridge, "Krista Got Clean," *Kensington Blues*, October 2, 2014, available at https://kensingtonblues.com/2014/10/02/krista-got-clean/#comments.

7. Clarence, personal communication, August 23, 2017.

8. Charles O'Brien, personal communication, August 23, 2017.

9. Signe Espinoza, personal communication, August 24, 2017.

10. Zoe Van Orsdol, personal communication, August 24, 2017.

11. Stockbridge, personal communication.

12. Matt N., personal communication, August 23, 2017.

13. Ibid.

14. Jerry, personal communication, August 24, 2017.

15. Stockbridge, "Krista Got Clean."

NATIONAL PASTIME

Lynn Melnick

Experience tells me
readers seem okay with poems about sexual violence

but more like sexy violence, which is to say

we want our victims with a cinched waist.
I'm getting a little bored with your ongoing fantasies.

Anything can be begged into art.

Most of my first wanted pregnancy I watched the Mets
on channel eleven while lying on my left side.

Much of my second wanted pregnancy wasn't during baseball season.
I watched a lot of kids' TV.

I cried every time Mister Rogers told me I had worth.

I love how a game unfolds slowly
how little happens for innings and suddenly it's all happening.

I love the relentless but practical hope of every at bat.

A literary agent told me that rape is hot right now.
Read my rape! Read *my* rape!

The other night I posted a purple sunset
only to see everyone else's purple sunset across my phone

until suddenly what had astonished me seemed tacky.

Experience tells me
editors want to read my rape poems

until someone else sends rape poems
that are an extended metaphor

for this ancient god or that well-known myth
and not a spirited description of what becomes of labia

when a man forces himself past.

What am I getting at? I have no solution, no vision
for the future. I can see you're turned on by my ruin.

(Words that are heavy with nothing but trouble)

What am I saying?

I'm saying: I'm not ruined, dirtbag.
I'm saying: we are no better, we who pretend to be better.

STRANGE BEDFELLOWS

Nancy Hightower

Narrative is a powerful force, so ferocious it launched Trump into the presidency. Psychopaths rely on storytelling just as much as saviors do.

White evangelicals who voted for Trump believed he was the earthly savior who would protect their devotion to the heavenly one. But just as those evangelicals cheered, sections of the church rose up in opposition. The pastor John Pavlovitz wrote social media posts about resistance, while other pastors used glitter ash on Ash Wednesday to support Christians in the LGBTQ community. Facebook groups such as Christians against Trump, Christians against Hate—#ChristiansResist, and the Christian Left, along with other evangelical organizations, gained more followers on Facebook.

The perhaps surprisingly forceful response of progressive Christians to Trump was matched by that of two other communities integral to my life. The secular literary world rallied with personal essays, petitions, phone calls, readings, and protests. *Entropy* magazine launched its "Trumpwatch" section, and others like *Heavy Feather Review* called for #NotMyPresident essays, fiction, and poetry. They were and continue to be relentless in their efforts to protect the marginalized. University professors also became more visible and vocal in resistance work as they anticipated how Trump's policies could affect the most vulnerable among their student population. I know faculty who created Facebook communities to discuss ways collaboration could happen across the humanities. Syllabi that focused on diversity and resistance were shared generously through websites and Google Docs.

We don't often think of them this way, but these three distinct worlds share a connection. They fight oppression with narrative because their very existence, their DNA, descends from a shared cultural history. Literature and the humanities are as immersed in religious text as religion itself. In that sense, they form a unique trinity with their ability to create powerful stories that last centuries, that can record, influence, and even change history. Yet I would argue that their message becomes lost in an elitism of their own making. A road so narrow that truly few can find it, let alone walk it. This trinity needs to take a hard look at itself so that it doesn't end up—through action or inaction—mirroring the false savior it wishes to oppose. Each community offers its own version of salvation, so the danger is ever present.

I know savior rhetoric and the multitudinous forms it can take, the way it can be shifted and shuffled so that evangelicals can feel like they are being Jesus with their soup kitchens and clothes donations even while they hold on to homophobic, sexist, and racist beliefs. I saw this double-edged sword up close when my father worked for three televangelists and my mother followed the charismatic movement, enrolling me in a Christian school and taking me to weeklong Bible conventions. On the one hand, these institutions provide a deep sense of joy and restorative community. When one of our congregation was sick, meals were made and delivered without a second thought. I could not have survived my mother's psychosis and abuse had not the church been there for me when I escaped. Prayers for healing and words of encouragement, as well being offered places to stay by different members, helped keep me alive as a teenager. Yet every congregation I attended in North Carolina, Texas, Colorado, and even New York City—whether evangelical, emerging, or Episcopalian—was mostly white, heteronormative, and middle to upper middle class. My white privilege made me visible to the church as someone who needed saving.

As a woman, I was supposed to grow stronger in God's word, stay a virgin until I got married to a man, and then have children. But by my late thirties, I was a college teacher who was still single, and I didn't want kids. Even though I still adhered to a heteronormative view of Christianity, I found myself on the outskirts of the community, rarely invited to dinners or social gatherings. I tried visiting other churches but found a disturbing sense of sameness—a mostly young, upper-middle-class congregation led by a white male pastor. I still believed in God; I just no longer believed in my church.

I found more multifaceted narratives in graduate school and academic life, where I scoured the texts of Jacques Derrida, Roland Barthes, and Julia Kristeva. Critical thinking became the promised salvation from a life of ignorance. There is truth to that hypothesis, as so many of us who were getting a master's or doctorate were working out our own horrific stories, hoping in some ways to redeem them. Yet a similar binary of us-them also existed. Instead of demons, we had the unread masses, the middle class that watched Fox News and voted Republican. There was no mention of the fact that all my colleagues were white, that all but one of my professors were white. My students were mostly white or were international students whose tuition supported the university. I wanted to be a scholar doing groundbreaking research on Henry James, until I realized that I would always be writing on one white male author in specialized jargon that only a few other academics would read. I came to believe that the trickle-down writing theory of academia—that scholarly articles written in elevated language will somehow shift rhetorical lines that filter into mass culture—is misguided. Just as Christians sit in the cathedral or megachurch, shaking their heads at whomever they deem "of the world," academics critique and often condemn popular culture from the ivory tower.

I moved to New York City in 2013 to be closer to the literary community. I had just lost my best friend to suicide, and figured I had to write my way out of a similar fate. There is a fierce love among writers that can make you believe in yourself again. The authors in New York—from science fiction and fantasy to creative nonfiction writers—believe that stories can work on the human heart in a way nothing else can. But the community can be its own kind of Narcissus, beguiled by a self-reflective beauty that becomes its own distorted mirror. Look at the mastheads of literary journals, and see if there is real difference from the conglomeration of white-men photo ops tweeted by the Oval Office every other day. Some promote the #WeNeedDiverseBooks hashtag that acknowledges this need, but when will we acknowledge that we need diverse gatekeepers as editors, agents, and publishers?

Understand: I read those editors and admire them, but where is the radical difference so often touted in the rhetoric they spin? It's not just the journals. Too many top-ten author lists, readings, and literary events are not as diverse as they could be, as I think many of us wish they were. The readings I attend are filled with mostly white authors—a choir preaching to itself, not unlike the church I grew up in. We authors are there because we believe that stories can transmit love, healing, joy, and rage. But we must face the cultural segregation we perpetuate; we lack diversity in our personal lives and maintain circles of white privilege on every level. I regularly attend mostly white literary readings in Brooklyn while I teach at a Bronx school filled with students from many different cultures, who lived in a borough without a bookstore until Noëlle Santos created a campaign to build one through crowdfunding. What new vision needs to be created in which these communities begin colliding and collaborating with each other instead of living on alternate earths?

If those in the literary arts wish to transform the landscape of America, they must become better evangelicals. That means publishing a range of diverse voices—not just a few well-known writers of color such as Roxane Gay and Ta-Nehisi Coates. We must invest in emerging writers from all walks of life, not just the "high" literary voice that calls out to its own. That means no more all- or mostly white mastheads and editorial boards. We must write and publish work that speaks to students in the Bronx and LGBTQ teenagers in Oklahoma. Make it easier for them to find us, or better yet, go to them. Create a crusade that rivals the days of

Reading Rainbow, and get books into the hands of those who can't afford them.

Because we're living in a dystopia under Trump, because the resistance needs all warriors right now, we can no longer indulge a pattern of redemptive elitism.

Writers have produced articles, essays, and books on how the church as a whole needs to embrace more diversity, but it was only after the violent Unite the Right march in Charlottesville, Virginia, that I saw pastors write collective letters denouncing racism. Some church organizations, like the Massachusetts Council of Churches, went a step further and promised to eradicate white supremacy and racism within their own establishments. Perhaps such declarations will encourage more clergy to investigate their own participation in systemic racism and spur conversation about the sexism many churches embrace under the theology of complementarianism, which says that women are to help men, never to lead them. Many, if not most, congregations are still pastored by straight white men whose sermons rarely deviate from a Western, teleological presentation of salvation that is always progress-driven and adheres very much—indeed too much—to ideology of the American dream. The church needs to become a sanctuary for all the marginalized, not just the "right" kind of orphan or widow; it must become known as a loving force, not the oppressive force it is seen as right now. Its pulpit must represent an American tapestry and not just the great white hope. Let Christianity become interstitial and intersectional, as it was meant to be, by understanding that the spirit of God can speak just as easily through hip-hop and queer women as it can through the Book of James.

Likewise, academia might actually have to destroy its own ivory tower to communicate with a world that still sees it as place for the intellectually elite, just as church is often viewed as a sanctuary for the spiritually elite. Less scholarly snubbing and staking out encampments by departments and academics would promote the kind of interdisciplinary collaboration needed to disseminate knowledge and foster cultural transformations. Let the high and low play together again in carnivalesque form; break literary canons apart, and let them be filled with, and overflowing with, diversity. Within five years, let's begin to eradicate the unspoken segregation in our colleges, so that community colleges are no longer attended primarily by students of color while research schools that boast of diversity remain primarily white. Stop believing the myth that English, philosophy, art, and humanities departments are diverse enough. They're not.

The religious, literary, and academic communities see boundaries and barriers between them; it's time to see the uncanny connection that makes them an interstitial trinity. We have such a long way to go, but remember that this trinity runs on narrative, on myth making. Imagine the power that would be harnessed if we began working in concert to become inclusive. Imagine no longer seeing the marginalized as people to protect but rather viewing them as the captains and generals we are to follow. Even the president and his corrupt administration could not prevail against such a glorious rhetorical army.

I ENTER THE REAL MEMORY

Alice Notley

The throne is up a sheer crystal cliff
I am the point of view *from* it   am only *I*
Then rise fly above all of it dark   enter through a
latched window square
Into . . .
This is my whole mind   I can't diminish enough
to describe your world now
The memory of here . . . I am that and its language written by winds
I am all of it memory language power   the green the pale
Green room must be midway back to the small world

Pull back to the green room   collage of crystal thoughts
have encountered
All you   I can speak to you here. Sound of
crystal static

I am conscious   of what you'd call my Power
I have it here but it is of being   and your tiny wretched schemes
Remain in their own   tiny wretched zone
In the green I'm closer to caring   and find The Old
Language   of fate   and the connection between there

and the world my fleshly body inhabits
I am all three   though the pale green room   be slightly fabular
And my location of The Old Language   still inexact

This
crystal has a forearm   because you and
I'll   very primitive notion of form an "arm"   I'll write

I'm standing on the highway the Real Mirage arms outstretched
small groups of soldiers patrol my "real" neighborhood outside me

In the pale green infinity the Fate tablet
    You are all and each inscribed
                         I stayed
on here when my husband died and I fell ill;
I had an apartment and medical insurance I have continued
slowly realizing the layers the levels of soulhood
I exist in; that having the capacity for so many
I finally might not be like others. I had assumed I was
similar and that it might be my strength to know that. It was
not so. I am like no one else—but the discourse of these
pronouns and of this difference now seems peculiar to me. I
don't know who you are. I know who I am who
my sons are and who the dead are. I don't know
what is relevant to this discussion, how to find you others, in
it. I keep being swept back even behind and above the room
of the fate tablets—this is one—to the sweeping crystal
transcendence. If I am not what I seem or am said to
be as figure enacting my life, then are you who you would be?
There will be more explosions: what is that to me or your
arguments about your religions? *I* am the one who
knows transcendence . . .
                      my palace or castle
is composed of spirit which is in a sense a thing
but the rules of it are opaque to science for its essence is ability
to collapse, de-structure, wander in and out of itself at will
in a timeless spaceless appearance or uncasuistic
happenstance, in which what happens are . . . say
mental tonalities in the hollows of words, spoken by
the dead. I had been trying to reach you one
said now I have.
                There has been
thunderous pain at various points in my timeline
such that I wondered how others might act usually as if nothing
much occurred, nothing transpired for them. It is that humans
have perfected the giving and receiving of pain, mental and physical.
If one speaks of evolution, they have evolved to hurt each other
intricately, elegantly. My parents never hurt me and I
found all social arrangements outside their household
shockingly fraught with injury, with occasions for
misbehavior, with the horror of the deaths of others, not to mention
illness and so on   that there is any reason to exist in this hellhole

of "natural" inflictions and abominable social arrangements
is unclear . . .
        I am on a cross in the Christian sense though
that be metaphor. Is it? I must be alive to save you purposefully
though I'm not clear how displaying myself so helps.
I have little faith in you . . .
           Pull back once more.
One of the dead told me recently to be prepared to make *statements.*
Before I was born to be on a cross I lived between the vast
Green room and the crystal exaltation   the tablets came into effect
When you left me we were all here together but you left
Is that a story or a metaphor for much of what happens
on earth have I mistakenly named a transcendent event
for human unhappiness? We were first all together one thing.
And then all of it but myself decided—and now understand
I also mean matter throughout the universe—you decided to leave
me. Or does that stand for, but what would you call it in some
new jargon or gibberish—alienation? No they call it marginalization.
And so you left and became this this, for what? To this day—that's your
time—you just die and come back to me, having suffered tremendous-
ly; is it some initiation rite, some acquisition of knowledge—is there
knowledge, something foundational to make you better dead?
I am on a cross; I am getting no satisfactory returns . . .

And in the green room where I also am there are warnings
on the fate tables   which I write almost without knowing—
of destructive fires, irreparable damage, the night.
If you just die anyway   as do I the human I should I
worry about this   the dead talk to me daily they are not dead
That life lived is too long for such pain
that you didn't need to be born since you were
already alive. That the tablets must be transformed en-
tirely, evolution smashed—the notion of survival called
finished. The notion of materiality *stricken from the record.*
You are and have always been spirit; your ideas about your-
selves are grotesque and imprisoning; everyone is losing.
I'm trying to get to you   but I don't care if I do . . .

On the fate tablets   which I write almost without knowing
and this is one
ALICE WATCH YOUR BACK   they now remember they left

but they are already mad as hurricanes crazy as swarms
crazed maggoty   or is it a fit to get back to The Old Language?
I promise you nothing. I am on a cross where time and space intersect
You come and go via me   the crystal exaltation
And the keeper of the layers of speaking and knowing:
You are in my hands.

PART II

SPEAKING FOR AMERICA

WHO WILL SPEAK FOR WHOM, AMERICA?

Edwin Torres

on the turn of control

What form will this take—the essay, the poem, the country, the man, the embodied reckoning with a language in movement? When did speech want to be *for* anyone? Let's dissect the *for* before *America*—who is in control, for the ride to arrive in? Who is the one stepping up for control in the midst of its lacing? I am turning a current with the only tool I have, as you, out there, witness the turn in action.

You, out there, will be who speaks. Turned up from this page, this writing, reached by allowing control to leave, to die, to reinvent itself. Clearly, there is no more speaking left. There is only you, left to define speaking. What will you speak of when asked, "What did you do when America lost its voice?"

What is the *you* invented by *you* that allows speaking when lost in *you*? Clever reversals of poetic immersion will not solve a deeply failed arousal; the treason attempted by a coward's incompetence will be survived by the followers of control. At this point, the form will re-form to speak on the equation of control.

on the equation of control

because most of humanity is a *feeling* and *human* humanity,
most of humanity is used to showing emotion, used to showing
compassion, empathy, honor, humility, human traits that characterize us
as human beings who understand another's plight, another's approach
in steps taken, not perfect, not angels, but *understanding warriors*
at peace with movement *through* sensation, *through* normal body functions
of attrition, attainment, pleasure, release, because most of us
are *feeling* humans, we get wrapped up when our human principles
are attacked and need to voice concern to make sure we're not alone,
that we're not trapped in our own image mapping but are indeed reflecting
the world as it unfolds, in that unfolding, in that slow unwrapping of
    control,

is where we expose our weakness and allow the shrewd maligner in,
evil is a fear-based weapon, to carve through sense and reason when
acted on without emotion, there is no binary feeling to power, only control,
the *feeler* is in need of allowing their *feeling* proper time to settle,
while the *unfeeler* readies another weapon, how to get into that mind-set
is how to lose humanity, the readying sword through the actions being
    thrust,
need to be equally *untimed* to match *unfeeling*, the speed of emotion
is a requisite fog that settles in, to understand its *unmatched* speed,
while the *unemoter* uses this speed as a weapon against emotion, building
    cut
after cut after cut, before the emotion bearer has sliced through the first
    layer,
walking through an urban setting as a kid, you develop a defensive stance,
a walk through the hardship that saves you, a lack of emotion that avoids
the trigger into external action while readying your internal attack mode,
you become a walking war machine through the neighborhood you live in,
the world you're presented, a walking time bomb, when your layers are
given exactly zero time to react, this is how to understand the mind
of a serial conscious-robber, a thievery of infant-belonging, set root
by the unrequited feast, how do you work with ugly fear, is there another
    kind,
spray-paint the symbolism, spray ain't the symbolism, spray-paint the
    symbolism,
thugs are waiting, to play the game, control speaks for who is patient

on the waiting feast

In seamless reparation, the Empty arrive
       in the midst of chaos
a formless fertility—dark as crude
       embers of a liquid nation.
Their genderless offspring
       a strangle of wingless subordinates
geared for unknown intricacies.

Who uses the word *sacred* anymore?
       Who dares give that much
to things you can't see?
       Maybe respect is harnessed out of tyranny
—the self-aware protagonist

inched by frame, outpaced by memory,
driven by a herd, stoked by a spill.

Winter freeze over the great plains.
How long the tome—for ancient enablers
to reach me, here, on this page?
Umbilical sky, reminds ribbon of its cut.
How do I form thumbs, to catch flames
enslaved by strokes
deeper than the cut?

on the formlessly enforceable

try to wrap your head around *taking steps outside the hole*, no matter
how enforceable your peace movement, life absorbs your trenches, *stay safe
be alert*, says the station crossing, claustrophobic, insular, mud-filled, dirty,
life gets trenchy, before the hole becomes the void, is there a realm
from within, a level to step up to, that forces *being heard* into
being understood, is that question worth balancing at the precipice of the
beckoning edge, as comrades fill the streets with individual displays
of human connection, the *feelers* emote beyond the trenches, I don't travel
with the trench lovers, but I know they're in their element, or am I now
fully trenched, there is another *they*, who look a lot like me, well versed
in the category of *other* I travel with, there is now a need to hone a DNA
that was always there, so I can look up from the trenches I've been thrown
in and find a way out, or make a new home, the ability for evolution is a
continuous mirage into the deepest wells of resistance, as a *human emoter*
every day is a fight to be heard, a civil uprising at our doorstep, our poems,
what are the arms we take up that leave oppression behind, what *sides* am I
seeing, to get this out of me, words as powerful *entitans* breathing for me,
who will speak for me when my steps are gone, taking steps every morning,
the *worthwhile* normal, the *changing same* out in the streets, in the speech
of the collective *real*, the *new* normal, mobilized, maybe the feel of
    escalating
change, is something worthwhile, something unavoidable

on the reliance of control

To locate your volume control is to control your obstruction. The catalyst
inside your dialed-in identity is what allows your voice to be heard. To turn
inside the *spoken apparition* is to experience America, turned.

To turn—to sustain movement—the shore's perception is that the angle is its motion to perceive. Its predictable center, the chosen core to radiate from. To land in the motion, in the season of the immigrant, is to silently speak your edge by diving below the outcome—the consequence of control is the form it takes.

The way to get past outrage is to decipher its meticulous trauma and surgically underscore the minefield out of its fortune—to speak in a language you can't be heard in. In our continued reliance on proportion and its relevance to movement, we equate our balance in the world we move in with a world we can't imagine. The ability to invent a size, a speech we believe in, alongside a microcosmic deflection out of our grasp, is what will prolong our nature as *evolving-feeling* humans.

In the season of supremacy, dialing in from the margin is how the *feeling* human sustains movement—to then, never land, devastating to the core. Every generation's obligation is to make sense of retrieval. Reigniting the center, to sweat the body, to curve down and speak up.

on the capture of clarity

best to keep lights off
      for the *seeingexisting*
boring a hole   into gut stasis—I left you
      a poet's tool sack
a combo genre   with no solution
      —to *churn* on your own
to *move*   'til you're gone
      to *no one* on your own

For the Nation

ON BEING AMERICAN

Samira Ahmed

You are seven years old when a grown man screams at you, spitting knives
from crooked purple lips: Go home, fucking Paki.

You are confused because the ethnic slur is inaccurate.

You realize, too young, that racists fail geography but that their epithets and
perverted patriotism can still shatter moments of your childhood.

You are the last to know that everyone else sees you as Other.

You keep your eyes on your paper and study and do well and stay quiet and
obey.

You get patted on the head and told you're one of the good ones.

You are a model.

Until you aren't.

Because those manners you once minded and that tongue you once bit
won't be held back anymore.

Can't be.

And what they think is rebellion is, in truth, survival. Because if you stay
silent one second longer, the anger surging through your blood will
engulf you in flames.

So you snatch their words from the air:
Terrorist
Rag head
Sand nigger
And burn them like kindling and rub the embers onto your skin, a
sacrilege, a benediction, a qurbani.

For the girl you once were.
For the girl you are becoming.

The one who doesn't ask to be recognized,
But demands to be known.

The one who presses into her fears to speak out. To stand up. To live.
   Anything else is death.

The one who learns that sometimes the enemy is a smiling neighbor too
   ashamed to reveal herself except behind the dark curtain of the ballot
   box. Sometimes your enemy is a friend.

You are tired of fighting for your name. And tired of the eternal question:
   Where are you really from?

You persist.

Because your name is who you are.

You weep.

For a land built on the backs of your black and brown brothers and sisters
   and soaked in their blood.

You claim your joy.

You lay your roots:

Blood and bone and fire and ash.

And in this land of the free and home of the brave, you plant yourself.

Like a flag.

THE BETWEENS

Cynthia Arrieu-King

I visit the state premiere of *The Joy Luck Club* in France as an American scholar with a French mother and Chinese father. My female boss says, *La petite! Aw, you dressed up so nicely!* I am twenty years old. I am invited to sit in the front row between the Chinese American actress flown in for the occasion and my boss. Instead, I sit high in the balcony and cry through most of the movie. Back in the states, all my friends say *The Joy Luck Club* made them bawl too. All these friends are white women.

My entire childhood I think there's probably no one in my city who is half Chinese and half French. But I wonder if there is someone half European and half Asian in my country. I think in ever-increasing geographical scales: city, country, continent, hemisphere, the world. It's as if some immense accident has happened that no one has seen that has resulted in my family.

A dark-haired woman stands behind a jewelry case of turquoise rings at the Hardin County Native American Pow-Wow. I size up the rings. She says, *You're Cherokee, aren't you?* I say, *No.* She says, *Yes, you are.* I say, *No I'm not.* She says, *Oh, but you really are.* I say, *Lady, I couldn't possibly be Cherokee.* She smiles and says, *Oh, you just don't know you are yet.*

My brother tells me my father told him never to marry a Chinese woman because they are guerrillas only interested in money. My brother's friend has a Chinese girlfriend who took all the friend's furniture and money and, turns out, is married to someone in China. I ask my brother if I am a Chinese woman, and he says, *No.*

The cashier at Lotus Food in Pittsburgh counts out my change to me in Chinese. I'm twenty-three. This is the first time anyone has ever assumed I speak Chinese. I don't. No one in the Asian groceries in Kentucky has ever made this mistake.

· · ·

Mei-Lynn does my hair, and we pretend I'm a famous star and she's a well-known hairstylist in Hollywood. I ask her to stay for dinner. When she sees it's a pot of stewed beef and hard-boiled eggs in five-spice sauce, she says, *My mother makes that!* I say, *Mine too.* Outside my family, I've never known anyone who eats this dish. I'm twenty-five. I have never felt gently happy in this particular way before.

My old roommate changed her name from Stacy McGregor to Flora Talaud McGregor to embrace her Filipina heritage. She meets her Filipina aunts and uncles and a cousin, Alice, who used to be the highest-paid actress in the Philippines. Alice was given shaboo (cocaine) as an actress to keep her thin, and now she has to keep thin by eating only mango, apples, and papayas. I have a cousin in Paris who is an actress in the national theater. She's chubby and looks Italian.

. . .

I find poetry by a poet also named Cindy King, but she's from Huntington, Alabama. I change my pen name to Cynthia Arrieu-King. Flora asks why I don't change it to Cindy Arrieu-Jien. I say, *No one will know it's me.*
I tell my best friend, Margaret, descendent of Pocahontas and thirteen generations of German English Irish Kentuckians, about this. She snorts, *Why don't you just call yourself Chicky Wang?*

My grandfather was a Chinese ambassador to Belgium. He changed his last name to King while there. He didn't want to be Mr. Chien, anybody's Mr. Dog. But this could be more legend than truth. Later a Chinese American poet I meet complains about privileged poets with diplomats for relatives who never knew what it was like to have to argue with their parents that it is worth it to go to college.

My professor, a woman raised in Pakistan and Britain, is asked by an Asian American writer if she'd like to sit in on an Asian American workshop. *No,* my teacher replied. *But don't you feel like an Asian American?* the writer asked her. My professor tells me the story and says, *Sitting around talking about all your little hurts—what a fucking self-indulgent little activity.*

. . .

Flora tells my friends at dinner about the deformations pesticides cause in migrant workers and the dangers of dairy products. Two nights later she comes home drunk and high. She says, *These are pretty playing cards. Where are they from?* I say, *France.* She says, *Oh, they're so beautiful, but you wouldn't want them to be French, would you? You would want them to be* American, *you're just* American, *right? Not Chinese.*

In the third grade Matt Philpot runs up behind me, shoves a xylophone mallet up under my skirt and between my legs and says, *Hey, chink, your daddy's just a chink.* Years later I see him at Revco. He is a polite burly social worker and rides a Harley Davidson. As we part, I tell him to take care.

Flora makes a movie about the Spanish-American War in the Philippines. To help her get it right, I watch it over and over. On the narration track, she says, "Someone asked me why I should tell this story—me, who is not wholly Filipina. Because I am the child of both perpetrator and victim."

Flora is forty and brilliant and twenty-three-year-old me can't believe I have to tell her to recut the pan of people crowding on a boat so it's synchronized with the voice-over about going away on a journey. Why have a Ph.D. if you don't know the basics of image vis à vis words? That people don't hear as fast as they see? That they look and decide according to expectations? That she will apologize profusely for a dish of mine she broke and I say don't worry, it cost forty cents at a thrift store. That it is twenty years later and I am still thinking about what it means to be perpetrator and victim.

. . .

My father came to the States when he was nineteen and taught chemistry at Columbia and Cornell. My father tells his friend that my students in Pittsburgh seem surprised that I know English so well, that they harass me. Not one of my students has ever said such a thing: I have never said such a thing to my father.

During the first year of grad school, my friend Caroline, half Jewish, half black, consistently brings me food when I'm sick, talks to me when I cry, and lets me wash my clothes at her house. We laugh a lot together. She tells me at lunch one day, *Oh, I was drawn to you especially because of your mixed ethnicity. I think we've endured struggles together no one else would understand. I wouldn't have talked to you otherwise.*

I tell my grade-school playmates not to listen to my mother because she's French, and French people are just stupid. I am seven. My mother overhears, sits me on her lap, and tells me in front of my friends that I should never say that again. She's never been mad at me this way before. I cry, but she walks away. It seems at the time like the most shameful moment of my entire life. My mother can't even remember this now.

A famous poet visits, and my Korean adoptee friend Jennifer and I drive her back to her hotel. Jennifer tells her about living in Oklahoma, about country songs and blood, about the letters written to her birth family. She thanks Jennifer for the stories. The next day at lunch, the poet signs my book: *To Cindy, thanks for all the stories about Oklahoma . . .*

. . .

My father says all black people look alike, just like Coca-Cola bottles. I write a poem in which all the Chinese people look alike, like Coca-Cola bottles. My African American elementary students try to tell me about their teacher, Mrs. Turner. *What does she look like?* I ask. In unison they say, *You know,* white.

For example, I say, *I always forget I look Asian.* I say that no one ever reminded me too much of feeling Chinese, just a kid in grade school once and some guy in college. Caroline says, *Why didn't people ever discuss your heritage with you in Kentucky?* I say, *They do if they're friends, but folks consider it fairly rude to bring up.* Caroline says, *Of course, they'd ignore it. They're Southerners.*

My white friend and I stand at the counter of a Chinese American restaurant with all the familiar items: mei fun, beef ho fun. Two children, one no more than ten and one no more than fifteen, take our order at the counter. My friend starts to get angry about the fact that children are working the cash register. He doesn't let it go once we leave. Out on the sidewalk I seethe, *What. Would you like me to call the police?*

When I am forty-three, someone with a Chinese father and a French mother, or maybe a French grandmother, friends me on Facebook. We do a reading together, and I say, *I always wondered if this would happen,* and Genève Chao says as she's introducing her poems that her parents believed in this kind of love, and now people are going backward, saying it's an impossibility. That we are people now, to some, is impossible to imagine.

"Horse in the Drugstore," by Tess Gallagher, has long been one of my favorite poems in the world. She wrote it from a list of words given by her teacher, Theodore Roethke: bruise, horse, milk, reason, bride. She constructed out of these random elements the story of a horse who "wants to be admired," who "no longer thinks of what he has given up to stand here."

I try to picture my father as this horse, standing in a new place, trying to forget. How he could not, though he never really spoke about it, how he often wanted to know why he had come to this country where they ask you how you are but don't really want to know.

I'm thirty-five. I make friends with a Korean American poet, Juliette, who laughs at all my jokes. When I am with my family, I am happy but feel all the sadness of growing up. When I am with Juliette's family, they joke, they eat, they talk about trips and play a board game about buying lumber and clay. The sadness of other people's families, other people's lives, unique and behind glass. Juliette and her siblings badger their mother to take a trip with them. She doesn't see the point, prefers to stay home and *watch the birds fly and the flowers grow.*

I meet a childhood friend, Tara, for the first time in twenty-five years. I can see from Facebook that she has been living in North Carolina, her husband has a farm, she has three teenagers, and she often thanks God in her posts. As I drive to meet her, I am not sure whether we will see eye to eye on the state of the nation and the world. I show her a photo of one of my students: I think Tara looks just like my student, though my student is wearing a hijab. Tara tells me she had West Indian roommates in college and how going back to a small Kentucky town afterward squeezed her to sadness, how her black coworkers asked, *What's your story? Why are you okay with us?*

The joy in Tara's face reminds me of so many of my friends from later in my life. As if the universe is telling me I've kept choosing the people who feel like home, despite all the paradoxes and strange exclusions, the ways of seeing and ignoring: how we survive when we stay near people who seem to really see us. That I've kept choosing that and tried to let go of the rest.

My grandmother hears I am visiting with this old childhood friend and says, "Tara—this was a long time ago!" And goes back to watching the television news. Every time it comes on, she asks me if the person who is president is really the president and then makes a shocked noise. She doesn't always recall when I have been there. Then suddenly she knows, though it's clear, too, that she has made survival out of a certain kind of forgetting.

One day a kid in my kindergarten class pulls out a tray of alphabetic blocks. He bothers me, but now I can't remember what he said. I go off in the corner to get a little distance. My father drives me home with my older brother in the car. He claims the school called to say I had punched someone at school. He is proud of me. I have the distinct knowledge this never happened. I have never punched anyone in the face, but I also know it's making my dad proud of me. I sit in the back of the car and say nothing.

. . .

My brother's daughter says she wishes her father would quit having a country accent, saying "y'all" and "Tuesdee" instead of Tuesday and so on. *Doesn't he know he was born in Europe?* He runs into people speaking French on the beach. He can understand everything they say and manages to befriend them despite his rusty French: he doesn't actually say a word of it to them.

. . .

The poet Farid Matuk talks about his daughter's night terrors. If he says he loves her, she screams more. If he says he's related to her, she screams more. If he says he will hug her, she screams more. She screams for half an hour every night. He realizes the only thing he can do is back up and be absolutely quiet.

. . .

I notice, growing up, that Chinese people don't think of me as Chinese. I tell my dad how they say I'm not a real Chinese. I feel stuck in a gray area between this reaction and the feeling that I am very Asian. My mom and dad keep neutral faces as I tell this story and advise not to say anything about it, not to let my upset show. *Le non-agir.* Have no reaction. *The one who fights is losing,* my dad says.

. . .

My friend Derek and I decide not to speak for an entire Saturday but plan a picnic to a remote Philadelphia arboretum. We take a train and have packed salads and lunches. We don't speak at all but write notes to each other. It's hard for us to coordinate a time to leave. It's so cold that when he leaves to go find a tree to pee near, he has to keep running around to keep warm. We miss the train by thirty seconds and pass the time by walking into a convenience store where the cashier is protected by a bulletproof window.

. . .

A professor back in the early 1990s takes his students to the Abbey of Gethsemani. They observe Vespers, the chants that happen regularly every day. A student gets up to leave. The professor later asks the student if something was the matter, and the student says he was freaked out by the complete and utter silence.

. . .

Decades before he passed away, Larry Hagman had laryngitis, and his doctor ordered him not to talk for an entire weekend. When the end of the weekend came, Larry realized he thoroughly enjoyed and was recharged by the silence and so arranged—for basically every Sunday for the rest of his life—to be silent. He'd get notepaper ready, make plans clear to his household and children, and just bask in the silence.

. . .

There's a massive flea market at the edge of Louisville in the early 1990s. A woman from Jamaica is looking over the wares at a stand. Someone says, *Where are you from?* She says, *Dixie Highway* and nothing else, doesn't look up, just keeps checking out the antiques.

. . .

I strike up a conversation with a man who wants a sandwich. I go into CVS with him, and he picks one and adds a soda. We go up to the register, and very loudly he says to everyone nearby, *White people don't do this. White people don't buy black people sandwiches. Count on it. This would never happen with a white person.* I don't tell him that my white sister-in-law buys food for people she doesn't know all the time. Then I think about the fact that she married my French-Chinese brother. To her, we pass.

• • •

It's 2015. I take walks in my neighborhood in Philly. I notice that for some reason it seems white people do not say hi back, but all the black people do. One day, a man with dreads riding a bike sees me carrying lima beans back from the grocery store and says, *Don't look down. You have to look up. Don't look down; the big bad wolf will get you. Chin up, girl.* And so I lift my chin. Whenever I see him, he says, *That's better* or *Don't let them get you down.* I feel distinctly that this is not something he says to just anyone, but I don't quite know why I'm the one to whom he says this.

• • •

My colleague, who grew up in a missionary family in Japan, gave up her marriage and law practice to travel the world by herself for eight years. She traveled in disguises and went to many countries in solitude. She says she got to the point where she was so used to being alone for days that she would try to talk to ants and get them to have a meeting with her. Better than nothing; better than no one to talk to at all. She remarks that when she was little, in Japan, she knew she shouldn't fight back, but when they got to America, her father told her that now it was okay, now she could fight back. This didn't make any sense to her as a little girl.

• • •

The comedian W. Kamau Bell has a routine about the fact that he must have a chat with each of his children when they reach a certain age about their being black. *Okay, so, this is why every day seems like you're having a shitty day,* he says. This talk is galling news to me, and then I'm galled again that it's news to me. I read that walking in nature can change the brain's health for the better. I think about articles on how black kids aren't taken camping. The luxurious value we put on either having proximity or having plenty of space.

• • •

On the American Psychology Association website, researcher Kevin Nadal states:

> A quantitative measure was created to examine the various types of
> racial microaggressions that people of color experience. . . . Thus
> far, findings suggest that people of color who encounter greater
> amounts of racial microaggressions are likely to exhibit a number
> of mental health issues, such as depression or negative affect . . . ,
> as well as physical health issues such as pain or fatigue. . . . So,
> while overt, intentional and institutional racism may have led to
> the deaths of men in the study, racial microaggressions may also be
> slowly killing the entire population of people of color.[1]

. . .

I come across a website dedicated to tracking microaggressions. I feel like I
am looking at the preservation of trash. Some way should be found to get
rid of all this ideation of wrong and storytelling and holding on. There's
so much else to be addressing. It is not interesting to polish one's chains.
But I know the effect is real, poisonous, and everywhere. Microaggressions
have to do with hearing and seeing well. Seeing others and seeing the self in
equal clarity. The equation is valid: that one loves or hates others as much as
one loves or hates oneself.

. . .

Watching TV one day, I see an Asian American couple in a cereal
commercial. They're in their home, eating cereal so cheerfully it's hilarious.
Aren't all people in cereal commercials cheerful? I laugh out loud and so
hard that I fall over on the sofa. I'm dumbfounded. There's no one around
to tell that there are Asians in a network television commercial. I'm pretty
sure they were eating Cheerios.

. . .

One day I notice a YouTube video of children watching a Cheerios commercial
that features an interracial couple. In the commercial a little girl asks her
mom, who is white, if Cheerios is supposed to help people's hearts. The mom
essentially says yes. The black dad is lying on the couch, and his daughter
pours Cheerios on his chest. Apparently so many people were incensed, in
2010, that an interracial couple was featured in a Cheerios commercial that
someone put children up to watching it and asked each to guess why people
were mad about the commercial. The children were completely stumped.

. . .

I sit in the armchair in my mother's living room, and the interracial
Cheerios commercial comes on. My white mom married a Chinese man in

1960 in Europe. I turn to my mom and say, *Oh, Mom, people got really mad about this commercial. Can you guess why?* She looks at the screen carefully. *I don't know; she's a nice little girl. Hm. The dad is fat? Is that why they're mad?*

. . .

I watch *Jeopardy* with my mom. She often points to a contestant and says they look like so and so, always some friend of the family or a neighbor. I'm struck by the fact that I cannot see these resemblances straight off or at all. Sometimes they seem tangential. She sees in a random face someone she knows.

. . .

I step onto the subway in New York City, and I'm suddenly overwhelmed by the feeling that every person is someone I know from the past. That they are all about to recognize me and tell me how we met. At the end of the line, I step out of the concourse to the hall where people wait for visitors at John F. Kennedy Airport: I see all the brown people pressed up against the railing, waiting with flowers. On seeing their faces I think, *This is my country, feel safe,* though none of them will recognize me. At the same time, I lose the anxiety I feel around white people's perceptions and expectations.

. . .

I sit in a waiting room one day and read an article in *People* about face blindness. It's a phenomenon of the mind: certain people cannot identify people by their faces. I reflect on the fact that no one can tell my brothers apart when they're on the phone. Sometimes people ask if I look like my brothers. I say the one that looks like me looks like a half-Asian Colin Powell, and the other one looks like a vaguely Mexican Tom Hanks or a white Denzel Washington.

. . .

My mother and I watch *Sense and Sensibility* almost every time I come home—about four times a year. There's a scene when Elinor and her sister, Marianne, find out that Elinor's suitor, Edward Ferrars, has gotten married to someone else. Marianne says, "Always resignation and acceptance. Always prudence and honor and duty. Elinor, where is your heart?" "What do you know of my heart?" Elinor spits back. The first time I see this scene, I cry. Eventually, after many screenings, I come to squint at Elinor and Marianne's mesmerizing teal-blue dresses and try to decide what to call that color.

. . .

An almost identical exchange appears in the Chinese movie *Yin Shi Nan Nu* (*Eat Drink Man Woman*), directed by Ang Lee. He wrote the script before he had ever laid eyes on the novel *Sense and Sensibility*. In that movie, the scene goes like this: "My heart was broken by Li Kai. And you probably think that I'm pathetic for never getting over it. But at least I had a heart to break. I don't need your pity. And what do you know of my heart?"

NOTE

1. Kevin L. Nadal, "Trayvon, Troy, Sean: When Racial Biases and Microaggressions Kill," *Communique*, July 2012, available at http://www.apa.org/pi/oema/resources/commu nique/2012/07/microaggressions.aspx.

THE ALTERNATIVES

Liana Finck

THE ALTERNATIVES

IDENTITY
POLITICS

WHITE MALE
IDENTITY
POLITICS

RIDDLE

Jericho Brown

We do not recognize the body
Of Emmett Till. We do not know
The boy's name or the sound
Of his mother wailing. We have
Never heard a mother wailing.
We do not know the history
Of this nation in ourselves. We
Do not know the history of our-
Selves on this planet because
We do not have to know what
We believe we own. We believe
We own your bodies but have no
Use for your tears. We destroy
The body that refuses use. We use
Maps we did not draw. We see
A sea so cross it. We see a moon
So land there. We love land so
Long as we can take it. Shhh. We
Can't take that sound. What is
A mother wailing? We do not
Recognize music until we can
Sell it. We sell what cannot be
Bought. We buy silence. Let us
Help you. How much does it cost
To hold your breath underwater?
Wait. Wait. What are we? What?
What on Earth are we? What?

A SIMPLE LETTER TO MY AMERICAN FRIENDS (UNA SENCILLA CARTA A MIS AMIGOS GRINGOS)

Carlos José Pérez Sámano

I come from Mexico. I had thought I was living in America before, but only since I moved to America did I realize that now I am in America again. For you, America is America, and for us, America is América, too. There is no difference, except for another thirty-six countries. Just that: thirty-six other countries, all part of America. I don't like to talk about countries. The world is one. Humanity is one. But it is impossible not to think about countries when you live in a foreign one.

Every single day there is something or someone that makes me feel "Mexican." I don't even know what that means. I don't know how a "Mexican" has to be. I am tired of having to assume an identity that is a mix of the actual me and their idea of me. I am a living caricature of the real me.

This has an unnerving effect even beyond everyday struggles with language and culture. Every day I have to figure out a hidden rule. For example, you can't visit a friend or colleague at home or work unannounced. You have to set a time. You can't park wherever there is a space. You have to read four different signs to know if it is possible for you to park there. You have to be careful about calling someone black, but you can always call someone white. You probably don't want to mention that someone is fat, but if someone is thin, it is very good to mention it.

Above all, there are acceptable ways of understanding reality, and you Americans use euphemisms to describe it. For example, you invade other countries and say you're "helping them find freedom." Instead of reforming schools and the workplace so everyone has the same opportunity, you use "affirmative action" to make it sound as if the problem is solved. These euphemisms are normal for you, as it is normal to call this country America. I only wish you were conscious that in doing so, you're ignoring the other countries that are also part of America.

Maybe this conceit of "America" is that it's a place for anyone. America, then, is a kind state of mind. I am impressed by the diversity this has created. I can't believe how many different political perspectives you can find in this country. There are people from countries that I didn't know existed. Music and sounds that I never heard before. Food of such variety that I get lost in the supermarket, as if I'm negotiating many countries in one. But the diversity gives some people a false sense of knowing and from that a posture of superiority. I talk to some people who sound like they know more than me about my own country, about the very things that I thought I knew best.

How can I explain to an American friend that, yes, all the world is here, but there are many worlds outside this beautiful and complex country? How can I explain that in my America there are another thirty-six countries?

If those countries—if all the world—are part of your America, why do I wake up every morning worried that I'll offend you if I hug and kiss you when I meet you? When will I feel free to ask questions without fear of sounding politically incorrect?

For more than ten years I tried to share my passion for literature in Mexico, and all I found were aggressive people trying to put me down. But here, all I receive are invitations. It's so easy to join associations, clubs, schools, and so on. I've worked with an organization that helps young children learn to write and another that builds houses for writers. I've given several public readings of my work—in Spanish, English, and Swahili. I've received all kinds of invitations to collaborate on various publications. What is the difference? Maybe the difference is that this country is made of people like me, who came from other places, who had to deal with a new culture and, in turn, are contributing to it with all our little differences. Maybe one day it will be normal to hug and kiss people when you first meet them.

* * *

Vengo de México. Yo había pensado que estaba viviendo en América antes, pero sólo desde que me mudé a "America," me di cuenta que vine a América de nuevo. Porque para ustedes, América es America, y para nosotros, America también es América. No hay diferencia, excepto por otros treinta y seis países. Solamente eso: otros treinta y seis países que también son parte de América. A mí no me gusta hablar de países. El mundo es uno. La humanidad es una sola. Pero es imposible no hablar de países cuando vives en el extranjero.

Cada día hay algo o alguien que me hace sentir "mexicano." Ni siquiera sé qué signifique eso. No sé cómo tiene que ser un "mexicano." Estoy cansado de asumir una identidad que es la mezcla de lo que yo creo que soy y lo que *ellos* creen que soy. Como si viviera una caricatura de lo que realmente soy.

Esto tiene un efecto desconcertante incluso más allá de los problemas diarios con el idioma y la cultura. Cada día tengo que descubrir una regla que nadie me dijo. Por ejemplo, no puedes visitar a un amigo o colega en su casa o trabajo sin avisar. Tienes que hacer una cita. No puedes estacionarte en donde haya un lugar vacío. Tienes que leer cuatro letreros diferentes para saber si te puedes estacionar ahí. Tienes que cuidarte de no decir que alguien es negro, pero siempre le puedes decir a alguien que es blanco. No es bueno que le digas a alguien que es gordo, pero si alguien es flaco, o flaca, es muy bueno que lo menciones.

Sobre todo, hay formas aceptables de entender la realidad, y ustedes los americanos utilizan eufemismos para describirla. Por ejemplo, invaden otros países y dicen que están "ayudándolos a encontrar su libertad." En lugar de reformar las escuelas y los lugares de trabajo para que todos tengan las mismas oportunidades, utilizan ciertas políticas como la "affirmative action" (acción afirmativa) para sonar como si el problema estuviera resuelto. Estos eufemismos son normales para ustedes, así como es normal que llamen a este país América. Sólo espero que sean conscientes que al hacerlo, se están olvidando de los otros países que también somos parte de América.

Tal vez al llamar "América" a Estados Unidos, se presume que haya un lugar para cada quién. América, entonces, se convierte en algo así como una mentalidad amable. Me impresiona la diversidad que eso ha creado. No puedo creer cuantas perspectivas políticas se pueden encontrar en este país. Hay gente de países que ni siquiera sabía que existían. Música y sonidos que jamás había escuchado. Tanta variedad de comida que me pierdo en el supermercado, como si estuviera negociando muchos países en uno. Pero la diversidad le da a la gente una falsa sensación de conocimiento y a partir de ahí, una postura de superioridad. He platicado con algunas personas y parece que saben mucho más que yo acerca de mi propio país, o de cosas que yo creí que conocía mejor que ellos.

¿Cómo le explico a un amigo gringo que, sí, todo el mundo está aquí, pero que hay muchos otros mundos afuera de este hermoso y complejo país? ¿Cómo le explico que en mi América somos otros treinta y seis países?

Si esos países—si todo el mundo—es parte de su America, ¿Por qué me despierto cada mañana preocupado por ofenderlos si los saludo de abrazo y beso? ¿Cuándo me voy a sentir libre de hacer preguntas sin miedo a sonar políticamente incorrecto?

Por más de diez años intenté compartir mi pasión por la literatura en México, y lo que encontré fueron personas agresivas tratando de tumbarme. Pero aquí todo lo que recibo son invitaciones. Es tan fácil unirse a asociaciones, clubs, escuelas, y así. He trabajado con una organización que ayuda a niños chiquitos a aprender a escribir y con otra que construye casas para escritores. He dado varias lecturas públicas de mi obra—en Español, Inglés, y Swahili. He recibido toda clase de invitaciones a colaborar en diferentes publicaciones. ¿Cuál es la diferencia? Tal vez la diferencia es que este país está hecho de personas como yo que venimos de otros lugares, que hemos tenido que lidiar con una nueva cultura y que a cambio, hemos contribuido con nuestras pequeñas diferencias. Tal vez algún día será normal saludar de abrazo y beso a las personas cuando apenas las acabas de conocer.

UNTITLED

A COMEDY

Herman Beavers

> *Some violent bitter man, some powerful man*
> *Called architect and artist in, that they,*
> *Bitter and violent men, might rear in stone*
> *The sweetness that all longed for night and day*
> —W. B. YEATS, "Meditations in Time of Civil War"

A hand on a thigh, foot
on a neck; medals, false
testimonials of valor, ribbons
of demerit, a positive
opinion of oneself. Men's

yarns bulging to boasting, loin cloth
a possible scheme. House vacant,
pointed as lust, the adjutant's winded
pants, his dress blues
plainspoken as a sudden

ache. In crow's blood's
riotous pounding; the heart a clock
or a drum, what to say regarding the old
soldier's labile two-step, shell-shocked
to attention, tossing khaki shirts onto a pile?

With an arsenal sufficient to maim, to
mutilate, pain's aim is to teach;
our last edifice a rostrum
trembling with lies,
our scars scaffolding,

an obligation to talk
late into the night. Forget
the whisky and whorehouses, the

eyes seconds from
cataclysm or tonight's last call.

Shelving plans for in-
surrection, the warrior readies
an ambush, *in medias res*, Latin for *we're in*
the shit now, and we aim to stay. Don't
tell me the heart's not in

need of vexation; minus
handholds, forty-round mag at the ready
we gape into compunction's blank
space, John Philip
Sousa tunes roiling in

our heads. In war's comedic turn,
colors primary and unassailable thumb
the safety off, heaven's itinerary
tactical enough there's reason
to leave every light in

the shed burning, scrawl
across acres of black
pages with white ink. Fearful
of dancing alone, we come into
the world as weapons in an open-

carry state, our naked, un-
holstered bodies lit by the causal
music of the muzzle flash,
the soul's spent round
ejected, clenched in the

      flux of score-
      keeping's bloody weather.

PIGSKIN, BEAUTY, DEATH, AND A HUGGABLE RAT

Linh Dinh

225 countries watch the Super Bowl, but
Almost none play. Unfamiliar with the rules,
They merely stare at a spectacle. Of all
American sports, football is one that hasn't
Spread overseas. It doesn't translate well.

The amount of equipment needed excludes
Poor countries, which are most of the world,
But its very nature also precludes
Global appeal. It is nonstop violence.
On each play, someone is knocked down,

But he doesn't writhe and grimace, as in soccer,
But gets right back up. With padded shoulders
And helmeted head, a football player appears
More than human. He is a machine. A robot.
A mascot for NFL broadcasts is a hulking,

Dancing robot. Thick-necked and impervious
To pain, a football player is the opposite of
Your weepy-feely, pencil-necked intellectual.
The objective of each football play is to gain
Real estate. For tactical reasons, a soccer

Player often passes a ball backward, sometimes
Even to his own goalie, but in football, there is
Only the forward thrust. In fact, a backward pass
Is illegal. Gaining yards is so important, it defines
The success of each play and of each player

Who touches the ball. A running back has
A successful day if he gains 100 yards, even
If he never scores and his team loses. In no
Other sport is statistics kept of yards gained.
A soccer or basketball player can dribble

The length of the field or court without tallying
Anything, but in American football, each yard
Must be counted. This nearly continent-sized
Nation has always defined itself by expanding,
By gaining yards and miles. Settle the coast,

Then foray inland. Move the indigenous
Out of the way. Kill them. Half of Mexico
Was swallowed up, then Puerto Rico,
Hawaii, Guam, the Philippines, on and on.
Now, America has at least 700 military bases
In 130 countries. That's lots of yards gained.

Granted, there are no people who haven't
Engaged in territorial wars with neighbors,
But the United States' ceaseless reach is unmatched.
Much more than land, America invades minds.
There is scarcely a brain alive that's not

Constantly titillated and harassed by
American culture. Worldwide, people wear
Hats and shirts with American slogans
And words they don't understand. They listen
To American lyrics and babble American.

In Vietnam not too long ago, a woman asked if
I liked the song "Aleet Beeper." What she meant
Was "Careless Whisper." Whatever its title and
Whatever it meant, she liked that song. Also
In Vietnam, I saw "POLO" stickered onto a

Japanese motorbike. This man had Americanized
His modest rice cooker, since America was much more
Glamorous and cool than Japan or anywhere else.
Humans are warm; machines are cool. Notice
The ubiquity of "cool" to denote anything positive

In American English. Americans aspire to become
Hard, tough, and efficient machines that feel no pain.
More specifically, they identify with their car, a
Sputtering box that enwraps them daily and gives
Them personality and status. As he spends more

Time with his car than anything or anyone,
The American's confidante is his steel spouse.
Nowadays, it can even speak and tell him
To go to hell or the strip mall. Each year,
Car commercials dominate the Super Bowl.

Its main goal, then, is to push more wheels,
Oil, and by extension, wars for oil. Ignorant
Of draw plays and blitzes, even catatonic
Grannies in the Hindu Kush are compelled
To ogle the Super Bowl, since the empire

Exudes not just power but a kind of sexiness.
The alpha male demands vigilant attention,
For he's coolly lethal. You can't duck him. By
His lizard-blooded calculations or whims,
Anyone anywhere may be blasted at

Any time by a plane or drone, even without
Knowing why. A study shows that only 8
Percent of Afghan men have even heard
Of the 9/11 attacks, America's pretext for
Maiming and killing Afghans. Even more

Than usual, war lurked behind this Super Bowl.
Before Christina Aguilera botched "The Star-
Spangled Banner," Lea Michele belted "America
The Beautiful," so there were basically two
National anthems. Troops with flags arrayed

Behind these sirens. As Aguilera mumbled
And fluffed, we caught a glimpse of a grinning
George W. Bush. Our war-criminal-in-chief
Would appear again later, as would Condi Rice.
After Aguilera's last note, military jets roared

Overhead. During the game, we were suddenly
Introduced to Sergeant Giunta, a well-jangled
Veteran of our Afghanistan carnage. He stood
With other soldiers beyond the end zone, waving.
As has become customary, announcers thanked

All of "our troops" worldwide "for all that they do."
Earlier, there was a shot of American grunts
Enjoying the biggest game in Afghanistan.
America is gorgeous, but so is every other land.
None can match her in mass hypnosis, however.

In a 1997 article for the U.S. Army War College,
Major Ralph Peters sums up America's cultural edge:
"Hollywood goes where Harvard never penetrated,
And the foreigner, unable to touch the reality
Of America, is touched by America's irresponsible

Fantasies of itself; he sees a devilishly enchanting,
Bluntly sexual, terrifying world from which he is
Excluded, a world of wealth he can judge only in
Terms of his own poverty." And "The films most
Despised by the intellectual elite—those that feature

Extreme violence and to-the-victors-the-spoils sex—
Are our most popular cultural weapon, bought
Or bootlegged nearly everywhere. American
Action films, often in dreadful copies, are available
From the Upper Amazon to Mandalay. They are

Even more popular than our music, because they are
Easier to understand."[1] The further one squats
From Uncle Sam, then, the sexier he becomes,
For without an actual experience of America,
This country is pure fantasy, a fabulous rumor.

One of history's oddest ironies is the name Mỹ Lai,
Which means "half American" in Vietnamese.
Mỹ is "American." Lai is "of mixed race." If
A person is "Mỹ lai," he is half American.
Mỹ in Vietnamese also means beautiful.

In daily Vietnamese, then, America
Is the beautiful country, Americans
Are the beautiful people, the American
Economy is the beautiful economy, and so on.
In the half-American village of a country

That calls America beautiful, American
Soldiers killed roughly 500 unarmed
Civilians on March 16, 1968. Nearly
All were women, children, or the elderly.
America seduces, then kills. During one

Of Israel's episodic massacres of Arabs,
I saw a photo of a dead child wrapped
In a Mickey Mouse blanket. Murdered by
An American bomb, she would be buried
With her beloved American icon. An American

Talking rat accompanied her to eternity. Watching
The Super Bowl, Americans and foreigners alike
Are blasted with this message: America is
Bombastically virile and stridently fun, if only
On television. The seats at this spectacle are

Way out of your reach, even if you dwell
Right here, in the cartoony belly of the beast,
But your seats at home are free, assuming
They haven't been pulverized by the USA.
Though you can never be this cockily

Carefree and invulnerable, this immortal,
You're free to stare, stare, and stare.

NOTE
    1. Ralph Peters, "Constant Conflict," *Parameters*, Summer 1997, pp. 4–14.

AMERICA (AFTER ALLEN GINSBERG)

Craig Santos Perez

America, you've stolen everything, and now I have nothing.
America, $1.3 trillion in student loan debt, 2016.
I can't stand my climate anxiety.
America, when will you end your wars of terror?
Go fuck yourself with your seven thousand nuclear warheads.
I haven't had my fair-trade coffee yet; don't bother me.
America, when will you be democratic?
When will you take down both your racist flags?
When will you pay reparations for slavery?
When will you be worthy of five million indigenous people?
America, why are your libraries full of the homeless?
America, when will you feed your hungry children?
I'm sick of your obscene inequality.
When can I go to the supermarket and buy what I need with my political
    poems.
America, you and I will never be a perfect union.
Your reality television is too much for me.
You make me want to riot.
There must be some way to end your settler colonialism.
Snowden's in Russia; I don't think he'll come back; it's unjust.
Are you being unjust, or is this a national allegory?
I'm trying to Google the point.
I refuse to give up my high-speed Internet.
America, stop surveilling me; I'm doing something private.
America, the honey bees are falling.
I've been reading the newspapers for months; everyday a cop is not indicted
    for murder.
America, I feel sentimental about black lives.
America, I refused to enlist in the army after high school, and I'm not sorry.
I vote to legalize marijuana every chance I get.
I sit in my house for days on end and Netflix binge.
My mind is made up there's going to be an online petition.
America, you should've seen me reading Fanon.
My yoga teacher thinks my chakras are almost perfectly aligned.

America, I won't stand for "The Star-Spangled Banner."
I have indigenous visions and anarchist vibrations.
America, I still haven't told you what you did to my dad after you drafted
    him into your Vietnam war.

America, I'm hashtagging you.
America, are you going to let your intellectual life be run by Fox News?
I'm obsessed with Fox News.
I watch it every night.
Its white talking heads are always talking about what matters. All lives
    matter. Blue lives matter.
Everybody matters but me.
It occurs to me that I'm not America.
I'm taking bad selfies again.

Sea levels are rising against me.
       I haven't   got a polar bear's chance.
I'd better consider my adaptation strategy.
My adaptation strategy consists of two cases of Spam, a hundred gallons
    of bottled water, and a journal of unpublished electric poems that go
    one hundred miles on a full battery with twenty-five thousand charging
    stations across its pages. Not to mention the community orchards of
    prosody or the millions of heirloom words that grow in metaphoric
    gardens under sunlight powering five hundred solar panels of renewable
    joy. America, I have abolished carbon emissions; capitalism is the next
    to go. My ambition is to be the president despite the fact that I'm a
    Chamorro.

America, how can I write an inaugural poem in your fascist mood?
I will continue, like Elon Musk; my poems are as ambitious as his
    automobiles
more so, they're actually affordable
America, I'm selling loosie political poems for one dollar apiece on your
    bloody sidewalks; don't shoot
America, free Leonard Peltier
America, save the climate
America, Mumia Abu-Jamal must not die
America, we are Trayvon Martin
America, when I moved to Hawaii, my wife took me to a Hawaiian
    sovereignty event; they fed us local poi and luau stew and sweet potatoes
    for free, and the speeches were inspiring, and the hula dancers were

angelic, and the chanters breathed their once-endangered language back to life, and the sincere poets made me cry, and no one will ever forget how you overthrew the Hawaiian Kingdom in 1893, and our struggle will remain creative and nonviolent and joyful. All of us there were warriors and rainbows.

America, you don't really want another civil war.

America, it's them bad terrorists.

Them terrorists, them terrorists and them migrants. And them terrorists.

Them terrorists want to suicide bomb us. Them terrorists jihadi mad. They wants to take

our comfort from out our privilege.

They wants to grab New York City. They wants a caliphate. They wants our oil fields in the Middle East. Them sleeper cells in our cities that never sleep.

That not great. Ugh. Them force women wear hijab. Them needs seventy-two virgins in heaven.

Hah. Them will make us fast sixteen hours a day. Help!

America, you are post-truth.

America, this is the impression I get from feeding at Trump's Twitter trough.

America, are you fake news?

America, I'd better start fact-checking.

It's true I don't want to be a drone operator and murder people at weddings.

I'm nearsighted and a hopeless romantic anyway.

America, I'm putting my native shoulder to the medicine wheel.

U.S. V. T.H.E.M.

Liana Finck

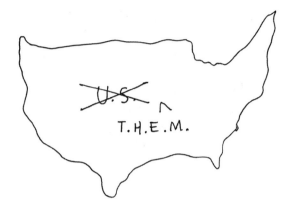

I WANT MILK, I WANT HONEY

Mohja Kahf

I want milk   I want honey   fresh in the comb
I want clean water in the river
I want green curling fronds pushing up from black-brown soil
I want a new world   I want the oldest truths
Cross-stitched into the breastplates of dresses
Handmade by Palestinian women living in homes that they own
I want the Israeli bulldozers set in backward motion
Unbulldozing their homes   I want the olive trees
Un-uprooted

I want milk   I want honey
I want laurel soap made by the hands
Of women of Aleppo and Antioch
I want sudsy healing in the bathhouse steaming
Women telling laurel-scented stories
I want the bombs undropping
Sucked back up five kilometers in the air into helicopter hulls
I want the Syrian people unmassacred
I want all the peoples unmassacred

I want clean water in the river
I want the genocides uncommitted
The pogroms unpogrommed
I want the lands uncolonized
I want the Scramble for Africa unscrambled
I want the Trail of Tears untrailed
I want the enslaved unenslaved
The Middle Passage unmiddled, unpassed
The ships plying backward across the sea
The raped unraped
The blood unshed

I want milk   I want honey
I want clean water in the river

I want the nations unmade
The empires unassembled
The religions unfounded
I want the Kaba unbuilt
The Cross uncrossed
The chosen tribe unchosen
The tablet of the law pulled back up the mountain
I want the holy returned to its home in our bodies
I want the family unnuclearized
I want the marital knot unknotted
I want the bad medicine we swallowed unswallowed
I want sexual union and limbs entwining
I want the wisdom we forgot   I want it back

I want to dig a burrow for the day to come
I need a shovel
I want to release the prisoners from prison
I need a crowbar
I want to release my mother from mothering
I want music   I want healing music
I want women dancing   men dancing   children dancing

I want healing herbs collected
I want to grind them with a mortar and pestle
I want cilantro and garlic simmering in soup
I want yams and plantains and corn
I need a calabash
I want rice and bulgur and nixtamal and couscous
I need a tagine
I want walnuts and pistachios and almonds
That we will spend years shelling and unshelling
Spending two thousand years on the mystery of the shell alone
I want the dough and the kneading of the dough
And the yeast that was lost

I want to make yogurt and drink it
Sprinkled with mint that I have planted
Cut, gathered on large round pans
Dried in the sunlight
And crushed by rubbing between my palms
I need sisters with minty palms

I need brothers with minty palms
I need a culture for the yogurt
I need the wisdom of the women of forgotten wisdom
Who know how to be free on the inside
And free on the outside   fierce and tender
Who are done with justifying the Lilliputian strings
That tie us down string by string
I need all hands to undo the done world
I need all hands cooking the feast to come

I want milk   I want honey
I want clean water in the river
I want a Song on my Tongue
The Tongue on my Secret
And Joy uncurling

.   .   .

Scholar Joy James calls Black feminism a "limbo dance": "In their progressive, forward movement, contemporary black feminisms often bend backward toward historical protofeminist ancestors like abolitionist Maria W. Stewart, Ida B. Wells, and Ella Baker."[1] This poem is my bending forward into what-if and bending backward into history for women's wisdom that was plowed under by industrialization, enslavement, development, colonization, occupation, invasion, democracy, capitalism, communism, and socialism. Can we imagine: What if? What if other worlds were possible? What if they're still possible? In 1889, Ida B. Wells imagined something held to be impossible: a world without the lynching of Black people. She fought until her death for that imagined world, which still has not come.

To do the limbo dance as a woman with Arab roots is to dance between invisibility and hypervisibility. So says Joe Kadi, formerly Joanna Kadi, the editor of *Food for Our Grandmothers*, which is the Arab American counterpart or younger-sister book to the formative anthology *This Bridge Called My Back*. Not all Arab women have Muslim affiliation, and not all women who are Muslim are Arab by ethnicity, but the Orientalist narrative affects all of us. Orientalism is the view that people who are not Western are inferior. What millennials today are calling Islamophobia is just one recent thread in the discursive web of Orientalism that Europeans and Americans have woven since European colonization of lands in Asia and Africa began.

As women with roots in Asia and Africa, we are hypervisible when perceived as victims who need saving by Western invasions of countries with Muslim majorities. Or when a Muslim American woman enters a U.S. store with her male family member, and white customers ask her if she's okay and offer to help her to escape from him. The ghastly fact that the deaths by U.S. bombing of women who are Muslim, in invasions coded as liberating Muslim women, generally go unnoticed by these same saviors is enough to describe our invisibility. Other examples of our invisibility include when I go to a U.S. bank to apply for a mortgage, and the loan officer tries to wrap up the application after taking my husband's income information without a word about my own income. Or when my credentialed presence as interpreter for an Arabic-speaking refugee in a U.S. hospital is ignored. Or every time a Syrian refugee is subjected to a medical procedure to which she did not give informed consent. Our invisibility is also evident in that the fact that women have been elected as heads of state in half a dozen Muslim-majority countries never seems to make an imprint in American pop culture, while the fact that women cannot drive in one Muslim country in the world seems known to every American. Both hypervisibility and invisibility deny our agency.

What if we limbo dance to resist this? Adding a different dimension to Joy James's version of the limbo dance that blends past and present, our variety of the dance is a dual critique aimed at both Western Orientalism and Arab sexism. We resist both external systemic racism and gender injustice within our own communities and all the entanglements of both with ethnicity, class, heteronormativity, and power. This multiple motion of resisting internal and external oppression simultaneously is deeply familiar to U.S. women of color. Women of color lead the struggle in the United States against injustice done *to* our communities of belonging, as well as the struggle against gender injustice, homophobia, and transphobia *within* our communities.

Linking arms *across* our minority communities is another dance move in our repertoire. It is time to intensify that move, to multiply alliances that can connect our various minority communities with each other, to compare experiences in order to deepen strategies. Any wisdom we more recent immigrants have gained about the civil rights struggle in this country starts with Black people. It starts with indigenous peoples. This is a time for immigrant communities to develop increased witness of indigenous struggles and to take ourselves to task for our immigrant complicity with the colonial abuse of indigenous peoples' sovereign rights. Too much of my own past writing has shown too little awareness of indigenous struggles.

In our dual critique, this is a time for our increased witness against
the anti-Blackness that exists in our immigrant communities, be they my
Arab communities or other ethnic immigrant communities in the United
States. We, as Arab Americans, cannot expect to benefit from the wisdom
that African Americans gained in their struggles if we do not also hold
ourselves accountable for participating, in degrees, in white privilege and
colonial privilege, for aspiring to white adjacency and white proximity.
We, as immigrants from countries such as Syria, with the anti-Blackness in
our Syrian culture and with the discrimination against Afro-Arabs in our
Syrian society, must stand up and say, "Black lives matter." Send poet June
Jordan a message in the Spirit World: We got your message of Black-Arab
solidarity, June, and more of us are here to give back the heart-recognition
you gave us.

Jewish Americans are targets of today's newly emboldened racism
too. We, as Arabs and Arab Americans, must stand with them shoulder
to shoulder against anti-Semitism, even while continuing to demand
accountability for Israeli violations of Palestinian rights—violations that too
many Jewish Americans still find ways to justify, even though more Jewish
Americans than ever before are awakening. It is time.

It is also time that the bourgeois in my Syrian community stop
committing class oppression against working people, of their own ethnicity
and others. This is rife in other communities, too, but I am so familiar with
its particular shape among my Syrians—the rush to neoliberal paths of
private profit, the embrace of myths of meritocracy, the willed blindness to
exploitation of laborers—that this is where I must speak.

In witnessing, in doing the dance of dual critique, I draw on the Quran,
which says to stand firmly as a witness for justice on multiple fronts at the
same time, "even against yourselves, or your parents, or your kin, rich or
poor, for God has prior claim on either of the two" (4:135). The full verse in
Arabic is as follows:

وَأَمۡكُ سِفۡنأ ىَلَعَ وۡلَوَ هِلّ لِ ءاَهَشُ طِسۡ قِلۡا بِ نَي ماوۡقَ أونۡوُك اونُوۡمآ نَي ذِلَّا اهَيُّأ ايَ
نأ ءوَهَلۡا أوعُ بِتَّت اَلَف امَ هِ بِ ىَلوَأُهَّللاف اَرَيقَف وۡأ ايِّ نِغَ نُكَي ن إنَي بِرَقَألاوَ نِيدَۡ لِواۡلا
ارَّي بِخَ نَولُمَعۡت امَ بِ نَاَك هَللا نَّ إِف اۡضُ رِعۡتُ وۡأ أوۡلَتَ ن إِوَ أولۡ دِعۡت

Standing up for equal human rights across the globe and across
the board *sounds* obvious, but in every age there is always an excuse for
excluding this group or that from equal human rights. Oh, but everyone
knows *they* are thugs. Oh, but everyone knows *they* are terrorists.

When I ask my mostly white Middle East studies students what
the bloodiest continent in the world was in the twentieth century, I

get, "Uh, Africa?" The correct answer is Europe. Europe, forerunner in industrialization, nation-state building, and Enlightenment, was the bloodiest continent in the twentieth century. During World War II, twelve million women, children, and men, who had done no harm to anybody, were gassed in ovens, their bodies butchered for burial with calm methodicalness. This same continent, full of the descendants of those who once scurried across borders as desperate refugees, today stands as a gated community, kicking away the desperate refugees of wars—wars that some of those Enlightened nation-states also had a hand in fomenting.

Can we separate the concept of human rights from its European Enlightenment origin, coupled as it was with racism, producing slavery, colonization, and genocide? Can we recreate human rights according to our understanding of true equality, across race, religion, gender and sexual identity, and socioeconomic class? So that no one is hypervisible or invisible?

With every whirl of the hips in our dual critique limbo dance, we risk being misinterpreted in turn. Each side we critique attempts to capture the moment in which we critique the other side and freeze us in that one move and use it for their single-sided purpose. That is a risk we must respond to by counterstepping with ever-new dance moves.

And what sustains us while we dance? When do we get to rest our feet and to heal inside? Is the dance itself our healing path? Can we dance ourselves to queer old spaces to baptize ourselves in secret rivers?

Because, like the dance itself, this is practical poetry: I want that mitzvah, I want that milk. I want that honey.

NOTES

This piece was previously delivered as an address at the Toni Cade Bambara Scholar-Activism Conference, Spelman College, Atlanta, Georgia, March 24, 2017.

1. Joy James, *Shadowboxing: Representations of Black Feminist Politics* (New York: Palgrave, 2002), 44.

BLOOD AND SPIRIT

Cynthia Dewi Oka

Between them   a needle-drawn line
      fence of polyester   I stood under that flag

& sang like I was not raised under the sign of Else-

      where.   When America was out of reach

my father settled for rain the kind that steeped into the bread
      he rationed so carefully   *there*

standing at the bus stop kissing my mother good-bye.

Eventually he traded his life
      for a motion-detected driveway & the wind
kept raking our words anyway I failed

      as a warning.

He's gone now if I could I would
      tell him to enter America (future
tense) is to behold (& keep

      beholding) your face becoming

leopard, leaping down a red

      then a red

      slope   the passion of cityscapes prickling

      for prey.   You wouldn't have wanted, Pa, to wake for this

     . . .

In the morning, you forgive yourself

      for enduring. A spider crawls out of blackhairtangle.

A man who has not had a bowl to piss in for weeks broad-
     strokes the air of dinging iPads

for smokes & dimes. Demands loom, tusking

the pink sky; by noon, they blanket
     the park, the pineal gland,
     they make little ketchup-stained shouts

like autumn leaves. You weave past
     the bucket of black soap where pigeons float. Cradle
your father's comb, liberated from his clean

     fingers, his now-clean skull, you

mistake squares of light falling on your boy's chest

     for the panic of antelopes.

      · · ·

         Where did you come from?
         Where does your help come from?

         Why are you here?
         The ocean rolled to a stop.

         Who did you come with?
         The a cappella with no night around her bones.

         What is your purpose here?
         Was tired of eating my nails.
         Was waiting for my name among the rows in dirt
         peeled & peeled more uncovered each year no matter

         how rainy it got, the flag stayed erect
         like teak bracketing
                     the Smiling General.

         What is your purpose here?
         To acquire a taste for raspberries, feminism, recycling,
           Shakespeare.

         Business or personal?
         Where does history fall?

         ~~Is it vengeance you want?~~ Are you afraid for your life?

. . .

I left I was propelled by

a largeness like

all my forests had

coalesced to a single spot

on the leopard's

haunch

under all that starry

flood.

(The only leopard I've ever seen was

defanged.)

A dream you wake up

from, American

a love made

of tiny

alarms.

. . .

You drew blood, & the face under your hands unraveled like an eel. You were
confessed to: white teeth straight as traffic lines, under-eyes pink blots
like polluted dusks. You reveled, you were clawed to blindness, you would
not let this go.
She was screaming, farting uncontrollably; she was furious. What English she
remembered rushed into three dark holes   *you*   *shit*   *fuck*

The lights overhead not shaken. She waving fistfuls of your hair. You told
the policeman you threw the first punch. His eyebrows arched
in surprise: "You don't have an accent."

A thumb in a baby girl's mouth
in the shopping cart on a mountain
slope of Lay's potato chips.

Mother & daughter banned from the supermarket.
You heard Immigration paid them a visit, you
of the eternity of yellow-tipped bok choy & tins of Spam.
Face it.

In the train window's cake of mud & salt,
"I am no more afraid for my life
than of it."

.   .   .

Soft blue fleece between December's knees.

I watch the leopard pacing the kitchen floor (smacking his gums). I hear the
ghost in the grass.

I say, no, not today, maybe tomorrow, next year, depends

on the midterm election results. This is called "sustainability" or
"resiliency"

in the age of self-selected surveillance. There is pleasure & terror

in performing for each other. A line made of thread twisting

above me in the wind divides red from white:

blood spilled plus spirit preserved equal freedom, they said.

They, everywhere, is whomever we can least afford to believe.

I saw the ashes under my father's skin.

I put some of it there myself—it had to do with his red voice, how to make

something end. I'm thinking now of last summer, midnight, driving

with my Boricua husband & Vietnamese-Indonesian kid up the back of a storm to an Airbnb in the Poconos. Floodlights: a giant American flag

nailed across the front of the owner's cottage.

                                                          We tip-toed soaked

into the shed behind it, then dragged furniture to block the door.

Told stories about tomato-men & gods made of newspaper to stay awake.

It sounded like a diamond was breaking. I forgot my grief.

We have each other. The

each other we should have had.

AMÉRICA

Ana-Maurine Lara

Una mujer—corpulent, robust—
stretches her body
from the silver sun of the Arctic
to the blazing blue of Antarctica.
Her head arches toward Siberia;
her hips roll toward the bite of Benin.
She lies awake at night; at daybreak
her heart is a rising peak in the yielding
waves of the Caribbean.
In her mouth, she holds
the ebb and flow of bright waters.
The rivers that are her blood rise
from her lungs to pulse inside our flesh,
our flesh of fish
and bird, and otter.

I do not speak for América;
I cannot contain América.

The *cihuatl* holds me against her back,
the skin of me against her skin, a skin
drawn taught against the wind of deserts.
My breath rises with her aches and joys,
my heart seeking hers. I swim in her navel,
full of starlight and then of rainbows.
Her body, meadow and brittle bone,
a carapace and wings, is magical.

I do not speak for América;
I cannot contain América.

La vieja's rage gives way to violent fits.
Coughs draw her flesh
up into mountains; they shake loose

the soil from leaves of grass,
the bluffs shudder and descend.
The moon draws molten blood out
onto the surface, to stain the beds of lakes
and to cool against the sea.
The sun makes her thirsty.

I do not speak for América;
I cannot contain América.

Machines tear at *bibi*'s underbelly.
Her knobbed skin gives way;
like vellum it peels back to reveal
the tenderness of her.
They rub her raw. She bleeds,
sore and wanting
of nothing but respite.
She inhales. The wind
lifts dust from her exposed flesh;
our bodies are covered
in remnants.

I do not speak for América;
I cannot contain América.

Ki sa ou vle? Fanm mande, what
more do you want from this paradise,
this heaven of iron, steel, and coal?
Her bougainvillea cascade
onto asphalt at sunset; her mesquite
withers at noon; her sage brush
vanishes in a horizon of tawny wheat;
her cotton bolls dampen with the dew;
her cane stalks bend in the wake of hurricanes;
her tubers split open and grow,
and grow and grow.

I do not speak for América;
I cannot contain América.

Nor the vastness of her plains and pampas
Nor the evidence of her broken flesh

Nor the stretch of her waters and seas
Nor the grumble of her midnight aches
Nor the lushness of her forests and jungles
Nor the way her waters churn
Nor the beauty of her ice-covered limbs
Nor her many, many names.

For the Future

7.

LIFE AFTER

Adrienne Celt

THE GATES TO FREEDOM

Rene Denfeld

By the time I meet a new client on death row, he has given up hope. Years or even decades have passed since his conviction. He has been trapped in a horrifying dungeon, denied the most basic humanity, including being able to get a hug from his mother or see the sky. Often, clients tell me, in husky, forgotten voices, how they once dreamed someone would simply show up, key in hand, to end the nightmare. But then they found out that is not how the justice system—or oppression—works.

Investigators like myself have now exonerated over 250 innocent people and stopped countless executions. I have spent time in our prisons and almost every corner of our country. In the process, I have learned the truth not only about my clients but about the causes of violence, the impact of racism and poverty, and our country's path toward injustice.

What may surprise people about death penalty work is how basic it can be. It's not the *CSI*-level analysis you see on television, and it's not magic. It's diligence and time. I've spent months going through thousands of pages of court discovery, identifying witnesses and painstakingly locating each one, often driving hundreds of miles to interview them. I've crawled beneath overpasses to find the homeless and arrived unannounced at the gates of the rich. I've spent months visiting new suspects, until they are ready to share their most painful secrets. I've worked with attorneys who filed motion after motion to get key evidence released for testing. I've dug through dusty boxes of records in forgotten basements, knocked on prison gates, found translators for refugees, held the hands of rape victims as they sobbed, and once carried a box of diapers to a family living in a tent in the woods.

I've done all this because I believe that justice happens when the truth is found and brought to light. It might be in the client's employment file I finally locate, with a time card showing he was at work when the crime occurred and therefore could not be guilty. It might be the one hundredth witness I interview, who tells me about a story he heard about a cop who lied about a case, and that case is mine. In one of my recent cases, I found evidence exonerating a man imprisoned for seven years. Our team took that evidence all the way to the Oregon Supreme Court—and won. It took me over two years to investigate that case and to find that evidence.

Right now, many of us feel like my clients, trapped in terrifying circumstances that are out of our control. And like my clients, we are hoping someone will show up with a key and release us. But that is not going to happen. It's going to take us a long time to remedy the political crisis and to reverse injustice and inequality, just as it took us a long time to get here. But there is hope.

First, we need to understand how we ended up with a white supremacist as president and a Congress determined to hurt poor people and reward the rich. Those Trump signs didn't appear from nowhere. They came from our failure to deal with deeply rooted racism. They came from mass incarceration that stripped millions of black people of the right to vote. They came from sending at least one in thirty white men into prisons, where they are indoctrinated into white supremacy gangs and then released to spread hate in their communities. They came from one in four Americans now having a criminal record, representing a fractured country with deep divisions and an abandonment of our principles of liberty and justice for all. They came from inmate slave labor, which led to big-business support of private prisons—a profitable regime of oppression—as well as an increasingly militarized police force that offered union support to a demagogue. They came from accepting an economy based on oppression, from that inmate slave labor to revenue generated by arresting and fining the poor.

That's the way of all injustice: it is rarely a clean line with a single perpetrator. It's systemic. It's societal. It's cultural. Resisting this new wave of oppression requires a multipronged approach. We can't hope that others in a corrupt system will suddenly operate with integrity. Even if Trump is removed from power, the course we are on toward suffering will continue, and we will stay imprisoned. We won't abolish the Trump administration's injustice until we fix the underlying causes, including reforming our criminal justice system, fighting racism, ending the profits of oppression, and reclaiming our principles of liberty and justice for all. We do this for our own children but also for the children of those participating in oppression; transforming our country will transform them, too.

We are the ones who have to do the hard work, and the hard work takes daily dedication. The prison took years to build, and it will take years, not days or months, to tear down. The key to freedom is, thus, not our immediate anger, which blinds and distracts, but our perseverance.

We each have skill and passion to bring to this labor. We might volunteer to help refugees. We might look for local attorneys willing to donate a few hours a month to an expungement clinic, which helps convicts seal records that prevent them from finding homes and employment. We might foster needy youth, or teach inmates to read, or support human rights organizations. We might start new voter registration groups or tackle school segregation in our community. We might work at the state level, lobbying our representatives to dismantle mandatory minimum sentences. Movements comprise people coming together for change. Just as the civil rights movement had its voter registration groups as well as demonstrators, its educators as well as politicians, its artists as well as speakers, our movement needs all kinds. There is no hierarchy when it comes to activism. We all count, and we are all needed.

With hard work, our nation can find its way off this death row. We can live to see the days when the gates swing open, and we can all walk to a better future.

STRUGGLE

Liana Finck

I DON'T WANT TO
GIVE UP THE STRUGGLE,
I WANT TO WIN AND
MOVE ON

THE END OF THE INCARNATION

Malka Older

California was the first. It was dicey for a few months, with threats of war and loud talk of treason, but when some financial and trade benefits were made clear to the central executive, all hints of aggression were quickly walked back, as if they had never been.

The other risk to the hypothetical new country was internal. Towns, counties, and regions disagreed, wanting to remain or wanting to separate even further. For a while it looked like San Francisco would become its own nation, and for a few weeks the betting markets had separate Northern and Southern Californias as a favorite scenario, reaching as high as 10–1. The problem of where to draw the line between Northern and Southern scuttled that option, and the final vote led to a complete, single-state secession.

Texas was next, which surprised some non-Texans because that state had no particular problem with the way the federal level was being run, but once the prospect of nationhood was out there, a plurality of Texans couldn't turn it down. Texas voted for independence, then immediately established close political and financial ties to its old country, and went on, for the moment, much as it was. Montana did the same.

The states of the eastern seaboard dithered longer, believing size still mattered. Four of New York City's boroughs were fueled with a burst of righteous anger after California's successful separation, but that was tempered by the rest of the state, until finally the city decided to slice itself away. This proved somewhat messier than the other secessions, as deals had to be worked out around a number of cross-border services (New Jersey Transit almost went defunct), but it inspired (or shamed) Massachusetts into seceding too.

After that the rest of the northeast coast removed itself in irregular succession. The longest and bloodiest fight for independence was in the District of Columbia, where daily riots and the chant of "taxation without representation" hampered government business for months. The problem in D.C. was not only its prestige and symbolic value. When other states had separated, they had taken their representatives with them, tipping what was left of the United States toward a stronger consensus; D.C. had no representatives, no official opposition voices that would disappear with its separation. Finally, the ruling party convinced itself that it was an acceptable territorial loss. The government of the United States decamped for Kansas City and watched its territory shrink as its mandate grew.

.   .   .

Borders had always shifted over time; populations waxed and waned. Stars multiplied on the flag, and still we called it the same country; was it a different one now with fewer stars? Each of the new nations, as well as what was left of the old, tried to lay claim to the legacy of the original incarnation. This was easier to signal with a name than by demonstrating intangible principles. It was hard to call a single-state country the united states of anything, but there were several variations on "United Counties of _____," along with the Utah State Authority and the Unity State of Arizona.

Intangible principles were not ignored. The new countries argued they had followed them by separating; the remaining United States opined at every opportunity that they were truer to their values because they stayed.

.   .   .

As the interstates crumbled, and the information superhighway took off into an unregulated snarl, the so-called underground highway appeared to help those unfortunates stuck in the wrong states. Despite its name, the semiclandestine organization was less about physically moving people—although it sometimes helped those without the resources to travel independently—than about finding ways to get them across borders and legally settled in a place where they were unlikely to die from chronic lack of health care, institutional racism, avoidable poverty, police brutality, or other human rights abuses. The new governments waffled for some time on whether they wanted more immigrants or not, and for a long time the activists' job was to know which fledgling country was accepting people at a given moment. At certain times some governments required proof of voting or social media evidence showing commitment to principles they believed compatible. Others focused on acute reasons for requesting asylum, like harassment or violence. A few, wanting to demonstrate that they were, after all, the good guys, and wanting to grow quickly and rebuild their economies, based their immigration policies on skills and education. Most at one time or another tried to close their borders completely, although that was, in practice, impossible.

Later, activists spent more time working to convince people that no one should die or live a drastically confined life because of where they happened to be living when the country broke. It was a surprisingly hard sell. After the cataclysm of secession, many people felt they were on a boat listing at the waterline after a desperate escape from a foundering battleship. It seemed almost treasonous to invite someone else aboard, particularly if they were one of those who had guided the battleship astray. Then again, secession had once seemed treasonous too. Separately and in their various coalitions, the new countries began to experiment with laws and incentive structures that would allow inclusivity without leaving them open to another takeover of hate.

It took much longer for the principle of rights transcending birthplace to be expanded beyond the borders of the old United States. Some activists and scholars argued that the willingness to accept people from the former United States over the rest of the world proved that the concept of that nation—and what was perhaps its most salient characteristic, belief in its own exceptionalism—endured, ghostly, in the public consciousness long after it lost effect in the legal and political world. Adherents of that school sometimes dated the country's true demise to the moment when the ideal of rights regardless of birthplace was extended to be universal.

. . .

In the meantime, narratives slowly started to shift. For almost twenty years reunification—through treaty or by force—appeared as a major subject of every election. Eventually Ph.D. students began to ask not why the nation-state had failed but why the union of unequal states had persisted so long, and civics textbooks pointed out the danger of a single, symbolically adored leader, particularly one elected in an unbalanced, media-heavy, money-dependent environment. Some of the separated states thrived, and others struggled; some separated further, and others signed treaties and grew together, even at thousands of miles of distance.

Even as the inevitable march of history left them farther and farther behind, fringe parties urged the reclamation of the divinely ordained and exceptionally great United States of America, fervently agitating in their imaginary political space for far longer than the country of that name had existed.

IF YOU CAN KEEP IT

Veronica Scott Esposito

I would like to start by telling you where I come from as an American. I
was born and raised in a midsized suburb called Arcadia, some twenty miles
from the heart of Los Angeles, a sunny, tree-lined place that well-to-do
parents move to because of the high property values and good schools for
their children.

Arcadia is very different from where I currently live, which is Oakland,
California. Not only is Oakland quite a world apart, but the California
of 2018 has changed drastically from the California of my childhood. Let
me share a few stories. I remember one day in the fourth grade, we were
being given a lesson on the 1988 election, and our teacher polled us on the
candidate our parents planned on voting for. First, she said George Bush,
and something like thirty tiny hands shot up into the air. And then she said
Michael Dukakis, and one lonely little hand went up. It was not mine.

California went on to give Bush a decisive victory in 1988, and six
years later, in 1994, Proposition 187 was approved. The purpose of this
proposition was to exclude illegal immigrants from state services—most
pointedly, health care and education. It was a punitive measure that fed
on a tide of anger at black and brown people, regardless of whether they
were legally in the United States. This proposition passed easily, by a
margin of 59 to 41. I was only sixteen years old, so I did not participate in
approving Prop 187, but I would have voted for it if I could, and I did feel
hugely satisfied when it passed. In that same year California also approved
Proposition 184, the infamous "Three Strikes" law, which mandated harsh
minimum sentences and life imprisonment for anybody who was found
guilty of three felonies. This vengeful, illiberal law, too, filled me with great
pleasure.

I make these admissions to share that I understand the deep resentment
that has fueled the rise of illiberal politics across America and that has come
to a head so grotesquely in the election of a race-baiting, abusive demagogue
as president of the United States. I was born in the year of the great
California tax revolt—commonly known as Prop 13—and for the first
two decades of my life, I lived in a place where politics were dominated by
government-bashing rhetoric that played on the fears and angers of voters
and that produced policies based on resentment and rage. The Arcadia of

my youth had very few African American or Hispanic residents; I feel its lack of diversity allowed for the easy creation of straw men, fueling racism that inflected my political views.

Nowadays, when both I and the state I live in have completely reversed these positions, when I, in fact, find it difficult to fathom that I or anybody in my community could ever favor such heartless and clearly damaining legislation, I tell myself that these weren't really my beliefs. They were those of the community that I came from, simply the inheritance I was given as a Californian of a certain time and place. There is some truth here, although, obviously, it does not absolve me of my early beliefs; I was not a passive vessel, and even at that naïve age, I was capable of generating ideas of my own and acting on them. I simply chose to adopt the beliefs of the place and family I came from because I did not see anything particularly objectionable about them.

Where precisely did my community end and I begin? In 1996, I entered my senior year of high school, and I had been accepted onto the "Constitution team." Instead of attending the normal social sciences and economics class, I was placed onto one of six teams furiously preparing to participate in mock congressional hearings. We were to create a prepared statement on certain questions of American government and respond to extemporaneous questions thereafter. I was on Team 2, which specialized in the founding of the United States, *The Federalist Papers*, and the origins of the U.S. Constitution.

The Constitution team had long been a point of pride for my high school, one of the best public high schools in the state, even in the nation. No one would dare imagine that Arcadia High School's Constitution team would do anything other than breeze through the local competition in early December, and it was very much expected that we make an excellent showing at the statewide competition in February. We did, in fact, breeze through the local competition, and we did more than make an excellent showing at the state level—we won that competition and went on to the national hearings in beautiful springtime Washington, D.C.

This was my very first trip to the nation's capital. I can still recall the profound feelings of patriotism and national pride that took me unawares, welling up constantly as we toured the monuments and the Capitol, how seemingly inexhaustible and sincere they were. I did not anticipate these emotions at all, and I had no idea where they came from. It just seemed that something about my upbringing had instilled in me an extraordinarily profound love of this nation, its symbols, and its government buildings. When I saw face to face the institutions I had studied so fiercely for many months, I instinctively felt chills down my spine and an intense pride for this government that ruled us.

And as to the national competition? It was very, very stiff. My teammates and I shed many tears over those two days as we scrutinized every last word of our prepared statements and combed over the writings of our nation's founders, Supreme Court, and greatest presidents and national leaders. I cannot imagine that in the spring of 1997 many high school seniors knew more about our form of government than we did. And at the end of those two days, we attended an awards dinner in which we collectively held our breath as the winning school was announced. As it happened, ours was the second-to-last name to be called that evening—we ended up with a heartbreaking runner-up finish to an all-girls school from the East Coast.

During those several months of intense study, I came to care very deeply about the daring originality of what had been wrought, the mixture of idealism and practicality that had brought about a system unlike any that had been tried before, the men and women who had invested their lives in improving this system so that with each passing generation America came a little closer to its ideal. I also came to see my role as a citizen in perpetuating this system. At the national competition awards dinner, the speaker was Supreme Court Justice David Souter—shaking his hand was among the biggest thrills of my young life, though I would not have given much thought to shaking a Supreme Court justice's hand a year prior. I hung on his every word, and I have never forgotten that he concluded his speech by quoting Benjamin Franklin's famous line when asked what system of government America had adopted: "a Republic, if you can keep it."

Never before had I considered that our republic might need keeping or that I should bear some responsibility for it. For the first time, I imagined myself as a citizen of this country who had some substantial input in its fate. When I chose to study political science and economics at Berkeley, I built on this awakening and began to embrace a liberal identity. It did not happen overnight, and there was no brainwashing involved—in fact, it did not complete with my graduation: only in the years after I earned my degree did I embrace such an orthodox idea as that of government-run health care. It took me even longer to become an opponent of the death penalty. Even today I still find myself weighing out the exact parameters of what it means to be a liberal in America, and I imagine that this will continue for a lifetime.

I don't know that I would have become as civic-minded an adult as I am if not for my participation on the Constitution team. I very much doubt I would have gone on to Berkeley to study political science and economics otherwise. I do not think I would have taken such a keen, lifelong interest in the ideas and institutions that underlie the working of our system—in their origins, their evolution, and their continued health in my lifetime.

Aside from one fiery U.S. history professor who disdainfully remarked how outrageous it was that Andrew Jackson's portrait was still on our currency, I got very little ostensible spin with my Berkeley education. The university did not propagandize me. It gave me the opportunity to engage with thinkers whose ideas had laid the groundwork for the modern concept of the liberal democracy, those who had fleshed out what liberal government would look like in an era of universal franchise, centralized management of the economy, national income taxes, and mass communications. It was exposure to these thinkers, and the opportunity to have high-minded, enlightening conversations about them, that marked my turn from a conservative bent to a liberal one. These years gave me the tools to shape my idea of myself as an American citizen.

This is the broad outline of my political formation. I think it amply illustrates the profound effect that ideas can have on an individual. They are powerful things! Progress, community, rational truth, tolerance—they were the aspirations of those who put our nation onto the Earth. As long as the citizens of this nation truly adhere to these goals, we can respect one another's views, be they liberal or conservative. As long as these values guide us, we may rightly debate the means of bettering our democracy, but we will never subvert it.

When in high school I read the entirety of *The Federalist Papers*, I did it because I was seduced by the logic by which Alexander Hamilton, James Madison, and John Jay argued for a system of government that would perpetuate these liberal beliefs. When in the year after I graduated college I read Michael Walzer's *Just and Unjust Wars*—which made me pacifistic and laid the groundwork for my absolute refusal of the second Iraq War—I did it because a taste of this book in my sophomore year had shown me a way of thinking about war that I had never, ever imagined. I could go on and on with such examples.

Once I had gotten these ideas into my bloodstream, it was absolutely impossible to believe in such blatantly illiberal legislation as Propositions 187 and 184. Documents such as the *Federalist Papers* and *Just and Unjust Wars* are rich and inspiring—they have fueled the idealism of countless young Americans and have drawn countless immigrants to this country.

When I think of what it is to be a citizen of this nation, I think there is nothing more important I can do than to hand down these ideas to the next generations, as they were handed down to me.

What is the power of these ideas? Let me quote a little language that still rings in my ears, over twenty years since I first read it. James Madison, in the famous Federalist no. 10, considers one of the toughest questions of any democratic government: how to safeguard liberty while also protecting a nation from being torn apart by the factions that necessarily come about in a democratic government:

> Instability, injustice, and confusion . . . have, in truth, been the mortal diseases under which popular governments have everywhere perished; as they continue to be the favorite and fruitful topics from which the adversaries to liberty derive their most specious declamations.

Important words to remember at a time when fake news misled millions of voters in the 2016 election and when poverty and rage fuel the demagoguery that pushed Donald Trump into victory.

And here is Madison arguing for the separation of powers in another famous Federalist, no. 51:

> If men were angels, no government would be necessary. If angels were to govern men, neither external nor internal controls on government would be necessary. In framing a government which is to be administered by men over men, the great difficulty lies in this: you must first enable the government to control the governed; and in the next place oblige it to control itself.

Much more succinct on this same question, Madison says in Federalist no. 47, "Accumulation of all powers, legislative, executive, and judiciary, in the same hands . . . may justly be pronounced the very definition of tyranny."

I cannot imagine that I am the only one who feels a charge when I read these words; they go to the very root of our system. Reading documents like these, I cannot think in terms of Democrat or Republican, which are really just temporary constructs whose own internal definitions are changeable and contradictory and which fail to even achieve their frequently assumed purpose of representing the "conservative" and "liberal" aspects of America. These papers go far deeper. Quoted by scholars the world over, indispensible for guiding legal precedent and the development of this nation's laws, they are among America's unique contribution to the practice of human governance. These ideas are where we come from. They have grown and evolved with this nation. Our trajectory is to make them ever more expansive, evolving the idea of liberalism from its roots in the foundation of our democracy to the meaning of the term today.

And this is why Donald Trump so greatly frightens Americans on both sides of the aisle—his very manner of being, which is clear in his politics of resentment, aggression, big lies, and scapegoating of outsiders, is corrosive to these foundational ideals that we hold sacred. The very fact that so many Americans could vote for and continue to support a politician who is quite clearly dangerous to the very nature of our system is a tough reality that we must confront. It will not go away. In fact, history has demonstrated time and again that such situations will only worsen if nothing is done by good citizens.

There are many forms that the political struggle can take. I am most fortunate that I could read Hamilton, Madison, and Jay's advocacy for America's system in *The Federalist Papers*. Where would I stand without their light, their education, their indisputable passion? To recognize how much worse I would be without these words is to realize that I must continue to make them live. To continue to fight against the illiberal tide that Trump embodies, we all must find such documents and make them live. And we must also create our own. We must open citizens' minds to what is unique and noble about America.

Our system of government is premised on individual freedom, so it relies on voters to choose a government that will perpetuate our foundational values. This is the great nobility of our system—we may choose our own rulers—but it is also its fragility, for a corrupted electorate will choose ruinous leaders. Trump and those who have abetted his rise are extraordinarily skilled at corrupting the electorate, and they have worked tirelessly at this for decades. Trump himself is known for his media savvy, his rise on *The Apprentice*, and his strong ties to the *National Enquirer* tabloid; his son-in-law, Jared Kushner, owned the *New York Observer*; and his former right-hand man, Steve Bannon, went to Hollywood in 1987, where he learned to make lucrative alt-right movies and where he partnered with the man who would win the *Citizens United* Supreme Court case. Behind them are powerful newscasters, radio demagogues, and firebrand preachers.

These people advance a theory of an illiberal America that has captured the minds of millions, and the fate of our country demands that we do better than them. We must fight this as though we were in the thick of an informational arms race, for we are. Why is liberal governance that is based on the ideals of the Enlightenment better than autocratic governance that is based on strife, struggle, intolerance, and closed-mindedness? It is not an idle question, and it is not one whose answer is clear to many citizens who will vote for the president in 2020. Studies show sharp declines since the 1950s in the percentage of those who say it is necessary to live in a democratically governed nation—one survey has pegged the support of democracy among those born in the 1980s as low as 30 percent—and almost as many say democracy is a "bad" system.[1] The autocratic and murderous Russian leader Vladimir Putin is now popular among one-third of Republicans (up sharply from just 12 percent in 2015), who see him as a role model for America's new rulers.[2] These grave doubts in our system have not come from nowhere, and they will not dissolve of their own accord.

We cannot have nihilism, cynicism, or quietism now—only hope, vision, and engagement. We must create new documents. We must invigorate old ones. We must have the audacity to create ideas, images, arguments, and narratives so large that they will invent liberal politics for this century. Take the success of the television adaptation of Margaret Atwood's *The Handmaid's Tale* and the hundreds of thousands of copies that book has sold since the election. Or take the hundreds of thousands of copies that George Orwell's *1984* has sold as well. Sales of both books have been awakened by the present crisis. Why did it require the election of a dangerous demagogue for these stories to catch fire? Were they any less relevant to the health of a free, democratic nation before that awful election?

Even if you do not have it in you to write our generation's *1984*, there is still much to be done. It is not enough to simply share the news on Facebook that Hannah Arendt's *The Origins of Totalitarianism* is a *New York Times* best seller—we must read this book and talk about it with our communities. I have previously written about how independent bookstores have emerged as sites of resistance—use them. Ask to host a discussion, or start a resistance book club—you will be the spark of transformation in the lives of many people, and they will go on to change others. Buy a stack of Arendt's books and ask that they be distributed for free. Make a short film distilling this book's teachings, and share it on YouTube. Hold a series of teach-ins via your social network presence.

Be generous with your money. If there are publishers, or bookstores, or art galleries, or investigative journalism outfits, or other institutions that are waging this battle of ideas, support them with a donation or purchases. As long as we live in a capitalist world, it is a truism that more money will always make enterprises flourish. So give them yours, and watch them fight on all of our behalf.

Most of all, tell your story about the meaning these ideas have had for your political formation, and tell the stories of others. What were the books, poems, and essays that transformed your idea of yourself as a citizen? When did you see these ideas put into practice, changing the lives of people who lived under them? Such stories are so powerful—think of Trump's first Muslim-targeting travel ban and how it prompted people all across the nation to share stories of lives shattered and saved at our airports. These stories were instrumental in drawing up a tide of revulsion and advocacy that ultimately ended that ban and led to a judicial process that, at least thus far, should ensure a more humane immigration and refugee policy within the boundaries of the law.

We are at such a precarious, erratic moment that it is unclear whether Trump will still be president when this book goes to press and this essay is read. But it is no matter whether Trump still reigns, for the problem that he represents is far deeper. Even without Trump, the apparatus that has corrupted so much of our electorate will remain. There will still be the grave risk of another Trump—or worse. And so with or without this man to concentrate our efforts on, we must fight without stop to turn our creativity and compassion to the salving of this nation.

How will we do it? Be courageous. Be ambitious. Look to the good in this country to guide you. Today California is celebrated as the liberal stronghold of America, a bastion that chose Hillary Clinton over Donald Trump by an almost 2-to-1 margin, that is at the forefront of fighting climate change, that leads in marriage and gender equality, and that fosters economic and racial justice. But twenty years ago, I cheered as the people of this state overwhelmingly chose illiberal, intolerant, vengeful policies and elected a governor who promulgated such views. How did such a transformation take place in this state? What about it can help us reverse our national course, today?

It is beyond the scope of this essay to answer such deep questions, but here are a few thoughts. Today California attracts far more immigrants than any other state in the nation, and it is also among the states that attract the most internal American migrants each year. I believe California is seen as a place of hope, opportunity, and optimism, a place where merit still matters, where people have a quality of idealism and will continually try out new solutions to common problems. In short, a place whose culture is dynamic, not static, a place where the common good can cut through ideology, though it be very thick at times. A place where people believe in the possibility of change for the good. We have tried out plenty of bad policies, we have elected bad leaders, but we have not let our mistakes define us: we have recovered, learned, and struggled forward. This is what America has always done, and this is how it has risen to be a great, respected, and leading nation. We as a nation have reached a place of grave error: we will learn from this new reality that besets us, and we will make this nation great again.

NOTES

1. Roberto Foa and Yascha Mounk, "Are Americans Losing Faith in Democracy?" *Vox*, December 18, 2015, available at https://www.vox.com/polyarchy/2015/12/18/9360663/is -democracy-in-trouble.

2. Matthew Nussbaum, "Poll: Republicans' Confidence in Russia's Putin on the Rise," *Politico*, August 16, 2017, available at https://www.politico.com/story/2017/08/16/poll -republicans-putin-russia-confidence-241701.

CHARLIE AND THE ALIENS

Ganzeer

I

When it was my turn, I took a step toward the counter. The clerk raised his hand in a gesture that suggested I shouldn't and then pointed to the kid standing behind me to step forward instead. And that's exactly what the smug little brat did. He just marched on over without the slightest bit of hesitation.

You might find it surprising that this memory is coming to me now as I sit in a cold, dark jail cell on the Moon with three other inmates, sharing stories about how we ended up here. Like campers around a campfire sharing ghost stories, except all the stories are supposedly true, and the thing we're gathered around is not a fire but a shared sense of camaraderie. Much like a campfire, it's this camaraderie that gives us a sense of security. When you first set foot in prison, you assume that everyone there must be bad, real bad. That no one there is anything like you. Which contradicts a popular saying we have on my home planet, Capulanos: "If to prison you are sent, then for sure you are innocent."

I used to think it was just that: a saying, a proverb. It might've been true a very long time ago, when the justice system was anything but just. Or maybe it happened to catch on because it rhymes, and our brains are weak, easily malleable things incapable of standing firm against the irresistible power of the jingle. That may be one of the reasons I fell for Earth, a planet that boasts a great many jingles. Of note is:

Proud to be an Earthling
Where life is grand and free
The entire cosmos is burning
But here in peace we be
O the wealth we are earning
For our eternal shopping spree

In any case, the testimony of two of these fellas—a Menos-Earthling and an Aradis-Earthling—leads me to believe that there may be some truth to that Capulanos proverb after all. Both have ended up here by way of completely convoluted circumstances. The third inmate has yet to speak, but he's the one I'm most excited to hear from because—dig this—he's Human. I don't know about you, but I've never seen a Human Being before, despite having lived on Earth for several years.

Before Earth, I lived on Capulanos, where I was born. And it was there on Capulanos, when I was still a child, that I walked into Ziggy's Starscone Store—steps away from getting the most succulent, luscious starscone you could ever dream of—and got my first taste of discrimination. The clerk gave this fat little punk-ass foreigner preferential treatment. Not only did he ask him to step forward when it wasn't yet his turn, but he covered the kid's starscone in a thick blanket of Magic Sparkles. *Without charging him!* I saw it with my own three eyes. The kid then walked out of the store to reunite with his parents, obviously tourists. They had scaly skin and metallic accessories most peculiar in design, and the mother was lavishly overdressed. These weren't just any tourists: they were from the wealthiest planet in the galaxy, Earth. (But not Human, mind you. I'll get to that later.)

The clerk, less giddy than he was a second ago, asked me, "Whaddya want, kid?" and when I told him, he gave me exactly what I wanted but with very little interest. He lacked a certain oomph in his manners, which I wouldn't have noticed had he not been on top of the world to serve the kid who had just preceded me. The kid who most certainly should *not* have preceded me. When I asked the clerk if I could get a topping of Magic Sparkles, only then did he smile, but it was more of a smirk. He told me it would cost extra. With utmost entitlement and a bloated chest, I pointed out that the other kid had just gotten Magic Sparkles for free. A most unpleasant laugh escaped him, and he proceeded to lecture me on the importance of hospitality toward foreigners. I couldn't understand why I was being treated as an inferior species on my own planet! And then I wondered: If I were to visit Earth, would I get better treatment than the locals? I couldn't help myself from staring at the foreign kid and his parents. The kid sinking his teeth into that thick layer of Magic Sparkles while his parents shooed away a couple of locals asking for money. Granted, beggars can be a little pesky, but those kids could have obviously done with a little more meat on their bones.

But more than the local beggars or the parents, I was focused on the kid and his starscone. He noticed. And I'm almost certain that what he saw was a boy glaring back at him with far more hate than the situation called for. Yet the foreign kid's reaction to this was quite bizarre. After barely a femtosecond of surprise, he smiled. The little punk smiled because he knew. He knew he was a privileged little brat and liked it. He took pleasure in it. For the first time in my life, I felt this sensation: a bulge in my throat accompanied by a cardinal spark of rage. A combination that I can describe

Starscone Boy. (Ganzeer.)

only as the thirst for vengeance. To this day, the sweet aroma of fresh starscone brings back feelings of revenge.

The opposite is also true: a thirst for vengeance always brings to mind the smell of fresh starscone. Which is why, sitting here in this murky, bone-chilling jail cell about to recall the story of my incarceration, I find myself remembering this childhood incident at Ziggy's Starscone Store. Because, let me tell you, right now, at this moment, I'm feeling mighty vengeful.

II

I revealed none of this to my fellow inmates, by the way. I wasn't about to talk to these badasses about sweet starscones and childish jealousy. No, I started my tale by recounting my arrival to Earth as an adult a little over three Earth years ago. My official immigration status was, believe it or not, "Threatened Alien of Extraordinary Ability." The term "extraordinary" might be something of an exaggeration, but I guess it's all part of the myth Earth has carved out for itself as a refuge for underappreciated talent from across the universe. And, well, I guess you could say that my talents weren't really welcome on my home planet of Capulanos.

I had already made quite a name for myself as a quantum imagineer, starting out with fantastical reimaginings of everyday things: pedestrians on alien worlds, made-up species of street kids, and details of fauna that've never existed, all designed in a way where you could almost smell them. But as soon as I started to create imaginings that included opinion, my work began to rub some people the wrong way. Their opposition culminated in a scandal over a reimagining of mine that I don't think was actually very controversial. The hot topic across Capulanos at the time was about whether it was okay for females to cover their breasts. On Capulanos, women traditionally go topless in public. It's not illegal to cover up or anything, but it isn't the norm, and there's a kind of social pressure to go along with it. Some women decided to challenge that—no doubt inspired by the influx of tourists, who had the tendency to cover up and viewed toplessness as, well, less civilized. Still, I believed it was anyone's right to dress however they mighty well pleased, so I created an imagining of two ladies standing side-by-side, one of them topless and the other all dressed up. An equal sign glyph floated between them. Not a big deal, right?

Oh, dear lord, I cannot begin to tell you the amount of hate I got for it! Not just from advocates for the topless, mind you, but from the "rebels" as well! Neither side appreciated being likened to the other. Each side saw themselves as better! And the mediasphere was making an even bigger deal out of it, and my image was getting far more attention than it deserved. Then, of course, men who saw themselves as guardians of the female tradition threatened me with death. Not just once but day after day. It was becoming too absurd and, I'll admit, a little scary. Especially after that time my cocoon was broken into. I had returned home to find the place completely trashed with this message scrawled across the walls: *Next time, we'll make sure you're home.*

That's when I decided it was time to leave. To apply for an immigration permit to Earth, where freedom of expression would most definitely, I thought, be more welcome. This path not only would lead to a good, prosperous life on Earth but would without a doubt garner me respect and dignity across the cosmos. The kind of respect commanded by those tourists I encountered in Ziggy's Starscone Store a long time ago. But boy, was I wrong.

III

"Welcome to Earth, alien," said the immigration agent, emphasizing the "alien" as she stood to shake my hand. This was followed by "Welcome to your new home." She wasn't smiling when she said it, though. In fact, I'm pretty sure she was grinding her teeth. Call me paranoid, but I'm telling you, if that agent could have rejected my application, she would've. The way she questioned me during the interview was most condescending. At one point, she asked me if I was planning on opening a starscone shop, given that it's something my "kind" is so good at. I told her that I planned to continue what I've been doing all along: quantum imagineering. I swear I could hear her laughing inside.

This is how it works: First, you enter Earth as a "Threatened Alien of Extraordinary Ability," arguing that your "ability" has put you under threat in your place of origin. Then, if everything is in order, you are welcome to stay on Earth, but you technically aren't allowed to use that ability, not professionally, until after your Permanent Residence Application is accepted. You actually aren't allowed to do *any* professional work until your application is accepted. Which takes a year at the very least, during which the government cannot supply you with a stipend or residence. You can apply for nongovernmental grants, but those are awfully hard to get. Trust me, I've tried. But I had no problem roughing it for a full year, taking odd jobs under the table here and there, because how else do you survive on Earth, right? It's an intentional conundrum they put you in. In other words, if you want to migrate to Earth, expect to have a little illegal activity in your file that authorities can use against you whenever they want. Finally, there I was a year later, my application accepted. But there was something off about the way the immigration agent spoke. The way she said "alien." I wanted to tell her, "Well, technically, you're an alien too."

Sure, she was likely born and raised on Earth, but she was clearly the descendent of Tethraxians who had migrated to Earth a long time ago. Museums and official texts claim that the first Tethraxians to arrive were mere explorers. Not being able to stand by idly while Human Beings, divided into states governed by the petty interests of individuals and tribes and political parties, killed each other, the explorers called on Tethraxian dignitaries to come and negotiate peace among the warring Human factions. Before they could do so, a Tethraxian virus quickly killed off the fragile Humans, who had no immunity to Tethraxian disease. (Of course, the Tethraxians would never do any of that killing intentionally—heaven forbid.) The Tethraxians acted as fast as they could and set up reservations where surviving Humans could remain protected from strange alien illnesses. As for the rest of Earth, Tethraxians assumed full control and proceeded to govern the planet in a manner that was far more progressive than before. So say Tethraxian texts. Sorry, I mean Earthling texts. (I'll explain shortly.)

It wasn't long before Tethraxians accepted immigrants from all across the universe. Aliens from Kumiken, Menos, Aradis, and many other planets flooded in and became Kumiki-, Meno-, and Aradi-Earthlings. Tethraxians no longer constitute the majority of the population, but they still dominate the political sphere. They're the only ones with the privilege of being called just Earthlings, and they still decide which immigrants to accept and which to deny. Like the immigration agent who welcomed me to Earth, a Tethraxian descendent whose ancestors stole Earth from its original inhabitants. Based entirely on that theft, she sees it fit to identify as an Earthling and see *me* as an alien. As she shook my hand, I began to question whether I had any right to call Earth my home at all. Whether anyone had any right to call Earth their home without the blessings of the planet's original inhabitants, the Humans.

I began to see this setup as a strategy employed by the Tethraxians to legitimize their own presence on Earth more than anything. If the laws of the land dictate that everyone is welcome, then why would anyone challenge Tethraxian presence on Earth? Everyone, legally speaking, is allowed a piece of the starscone. Meanwhile, the Human race's share of that starscone becomes smaller and smaller and smaller.

I am part of this grand thievery, but I brush off the guilt without a second thought because my only other option would be returning to Capulanos, where nothing awaits me but death.

IV

Like I said, my first year on Earth was spent doing odd jobs here and there, under the table. Then I received my Permanent Residence Permit and was able to practice my brand of quantum imagineering openly and legally. At first, my creations were little different than the things I'd created in the past, but then I was approached by a couple of well-placed curators to partake in a big art show about the state of politics on Earth. I'm assuming their reason for choosing me was to include the perspective of a newcomer, someone who would likely idolize Earth and see it as a place of hope and opportunity.

Little did they know that my work would be so scathing.

I put together a glorious show. I created pieces that illustrated how both major political factions on Earth are self-serving fucks. How they should both be dismantled. How labels differentiating between all aliens on Earth should cease to exist. How anybody should be able to travel freely between all planets of the cosmos, but if anyone should have the right to claim authority over who to welcome to Earth and who to deny, well, then it ought to be the Humans, who are kept powerless within the confines of their miserable reservations. It was a monumental show that dismantled everything everyone believed in and declared that "stability" is nothing but a myth; it can never be sustained.

Soon after, the authorities came looking for me. They presented me with evidence of the "illegal" work I had done during my first year on Earth. None of those odd jobs were shady, by the way—construction, recycling, delivery, that sort of thing. But because I was not permitted to work, it nullified my Permanent Residence status, and I was slapped with a fine I couldn't possibly pay. So here I am in the slammer on Earth's moon, paying my dues by way of forced labor. And some people have the nerve to claim that slavery is a thing of the past.

V

I describe the immigration agent, my first year on Earth, and the art show, and after murmurs of camaraderie from my fellow inmates, we turn to the Human. We all eagerly await his story. He introduces himself as Charlie and rolls up his sleeve, slowly, calmly. "I'm in jail because of this," he says. The tattoo is very odd in design, nothing I've ever seen before. A rectangle comprising red and white stripes, except for a squarish corner in blue, dotted with a great many white stars.

"What is it?" I ask.

"It's a religious symbol from Ancient Earth," says the Menos-Earthling. "What's the religion called again? Ameri . . . kanizm?"

"Yeah, that's it. Americanism," says Charlie.

"Well, of course, they'd lock you up for that, mate," says the Aradis-Earthling nonchalantly. "Aren't you lot calling for a big Americanism revival of sorts? Where you dominate the world, sell weapons to people to use against each other, and open shops across the planet that sell slow-acting poisons disguised as food?"

"No!" snaps Charlie. "Those are the extremists! We're not all like them!"

"Well, what does your version of Americanism call for, then?" asks the Menos-Earthling, with a tinge of ridicule.

"Three core values," says Charlie. "Liberty, equality, and justice. That's really all there is to it."

I can get down with that; I agree. The others do, too, and almost on cue, a light flickers down the hall. Only for a second, but that's all I need to know that there's hope to escape these walls. That this maximum-security prison isn't fail-proof, that if the lights are flawed, so must be many other facets that make up this dungeon. Or at least the possibility of other faults is there. Faults we can use to our advantage.

And that thought was enough for me to smell it. The scent of imminent revenge, the undeniable aroma of sweet heavenly starscone.

DREAMING IN CRAYON

Craig Santos Perez

My daughter draws a rainbow
on a blank page. Then a yellow sun
and blue sky without gray fighter jets.
Then endangered birds with gold
feathers. Then green land without gray
hotels and barbed-wired fences.
Then orange coconut, green breadfruit,
and yellow banana trees. Then a purple
school with a library, playground,
and garden of red hibiscus and pink
plumeria. Then a peace flag raised high
on a pole to pledge allegiance to.
Then a village of green houses
with dark-blue solar panels. Then
a dark-blue ocean without warships
on the horizon. Then green turtles,
silver fish, and red coral protecting
our entire island. Then twelve brown
canoes with triangle sails. Then two
stick figures playing in the yellow
shoreline. The smaller figure,
with big brown eyes, is building
a sandcastle, while I am dreaming.

BECAUSE CHANGE WAS THE OCEAN AND WE LIVED BY HER MERCY

Charlie Jane Anders

This was sacred, this was stolen

We stood naked on the shore of Bernal and watched the candles float across the bay, swept by a lazy current off to the north, in the direction of Potrero Island. A dozen or so candles stayed afloat and alight after half a league, their tiny flames bobbing up and down, casting long yellow reflections on the dark water alongside the streaks of moonlight. At times I fancied the candlelight could filter down onto streets and buildings, the old automobiles and houses full of children's toys, all the water-logged treasures of long-gone people. We held hands, twenty or thirty of us, and watched the little candle-boats we'd made as they floated away. Joconda was humming an old reconstructed song about the wild road, hir beard full of flowers. We all just about held our breath. I felt my bare skin go electric with the intensity of the moment, like this could be the good time we'd all remember in the bad times to come. This was sacred, this was stolen. And then someone—probably Miranda—farted, and then we were all laughing, and the grown-up seriousness was gone. We were all busting up and falling over each other on the rocky ground, in a nude heap, scraping our knees and giggling into each other's limbs. When we got our breath back and looked up, the candles were all gone.

I felt like I had always been Wrong Headed

I couldn't deal with life in Fairbanks anymore. I grew up at the same time as the town, watched it go from regular city to megacity as I hit my early twenties. I lived in an old decommissioned solar power station with five other kids, and we tried to make the loudest, most uncomforting music we could, with a beat as relentless and merciless as the tides. We wanted to shake our cinderblock walls and make people dance until their feet bled. But we sucked. We were bad at music and not quite dumb enough not to know it. We all wore big hoods and spiky shoes and tried to make our own drums out of dry cloth and cracked wood, and we read our poetry on Friday nights. There were bookhouses, along with stink tanks where you could drink up and listen to awful poetry about extinct animals. People came from all over, because everybody heard that Fairbanks was becoming the most civilized place on Earth, and that's when I decided to leave town. I had this moment of looking around at my musician friends and my restaurant job and our cool little scene and feeling like there had to be more to life than this.

I hitched a ride down south and ended up in Olympia, at a house where they were growing their own food and drugs and doing a way better job with the drugs than the food. We were all staring upward at the first cloud anybody had seen in weeks, trying to identify what it could mean. When you hardly ever saw them, clouds had to be omens.

We were all complaining about our dumb families, still watching that cloud warp and contort, and I found myself talking about how my parents only liked to listen to that boring boo-pop music with the same three or four major chords and that cruddy AAA/BBB/CDE/CDE rhyme scheme, and how my mother insisted on saving every scrap of organic material we used and collecting every drop of rainwater. "It's fucking pathetic, is what it is. They act like we're still living in the Great Decimation."

"They're just super traumatized," said this skinny genderfreak named Juya, who stood nearby holding the bong. "It's hard to even imagine. I mean, we're the first generation that just takes it for granted we're going to survive, as, like, a species. Our parents, our grandparents, and their grandparents, they were all living like every day could be the day the planet finally got done with us. They didn't grow up having moisture condensers and mycoprotein rinses and skinsus."

"Yeah, whatever," I said. But what Juya said stuck with me, because I had never thought of my parents as traumatized. I'd always thought they were just tightly wound and judgy. Juya had two cones of dark twisty hair on zir head and a red pajamzoot, and zi was only a year or two older than me but seemed a lot wiser.

"I want to find all the music we used to have," I said. "You know, the weird, noisy shit that made people's clothes fall off and their hair light on fire. The rock 'n roll that just listening to it turned girls into boys, the songs that took away the fear of God. I've read about it, but I've never heard any of it, and I don't even know how to play it."

"Yeah, all the recordings and notations got lost in the Dataclysm," Juya said. "They were in formats that nobody can read, or they got corrupted, or they were printed on disks made from petroleum. Those songs are gone forever."

"I think they're under the ocean," I said. "I think they're down there somewhere."

Something about the way I said that helped Juya reach a decision. "Hey, I'm heading back down to the San Francisco archipelago in the morning. I got room in my car if you wanna come with."

Juya's car was an older solar model that had to stop every couple hours to recharge, and the self-driving module didn't work so great. My legs were resting in a pile of old headmods and biofills, plus those costooms that everybody used a few summers earlier that made your skin turn into snakeskin that you could shed in one piece. So the upshot was we had a lot of time to talk and hold hands and look at the endless golden landscape stretching off to the east. Juya had these big bright eyes that laughed when the rest of zir face was stone serious and strong tentative hands to hold me in place as zi tied me to the car seat with fronds of algae. I had never felt as safe and dangerous as when I crossed the wasteland with Juya. We talked for hours about how the world needed new communities, new ways to breathe life back into the ocean, new ways to be people.

By the time we got to Bernal Island and the Wrong Headed community, I was in love with Juya, deeper than I'd ever felt with anyone before.

Juya up and left Bernal a week and a half later, because zi got bored again, and I barely noticed that zi was gone. By then, I was in love with a hundred other people, and they were all in love with me.

Bernal Island was accessible from only one direction, from the big island in the middle, and only at a couple times of day, when they let the bridge down and turned off the moat. After a few days on Bernal, I stopped even noticing the other islands on our horizon, let alone paying attention to my friends on social media talking about all the fancy new restaurants Fairbanks was getting. I was constantly having these intense, heartfelt moments with people in the Wrong Headed crew.

"The ocean is our lover, you can hear it laughing at us." Joconda was sort of the leader here. Sie sometimes had a beard and sometimes a smooth round face covered with perfect bright makeup. Hir eyes were as gray as the sea and just as unpredictable. For decades, San Francisco and other places like it had been abandoned, because the combination of seismic instability and a voracious dead ocean made them too scary and risky. But that city down there, under the waves, had been the place everybody came to, from all over the world, to find freedom. That legacy was ours now.

And those people had brought music from their native countries and their own cultures, and all those sounds had crashed together in those streets, night after night. Joconda's own ancestors had come from China and Peru, and hir great-grandparents had played nine-stringed guitars, melodies and rhythms that Joconda barely recalled now. Listening to hir,

I almost fancied I could put my ear to the surface of the ocean and hear all the sounds from generations past, still reverberating. We sat all night, Joconda, some of the others, and myself, and I got to play on an old-school drum made of cowhide or something. I felt like I had always been Wrong Headed, and I'd just never had the word for it before.

Juya sent me an e-mail a month or two after zi left Bernal: "The moment I met you, I knew you needed to be with the rest of those maniacs. I've never been able to resist delivering lost children to their rightful homes. It's almost the only thing I'm good at, other than the things you already knew about." I never saw zir again.

"I'm so glad I found a group of people I would risk drowning in dead water for"

Back in the twenty-first century, everybody had theories about how to make the ocean breathe again. Fill her with quicklime, to neutralize the acid. Split the water molecules into hydrogen and oxygen, and bond the hydrogen with the surplus carbon in the water to create a clean-burning hydrocarbon fuel. Release genetically engineered fish, with special gills. Grow special algae that was designed to commit suicide after a while. Spray billions of nanotech balls into her. And a few other things. Now, we had to clean up the aftereffects of all those failed solutions while also helping the sea let go of all that CO_2 from before.

The only way was the slow way. We pumped ocean water through our special enzyme store and then through a series of filters, until what came out the other end was clear and oxygen-rich. The waste we separated out and disposed of. Some of it became raw materials for shoe soles and roof tiles. Some of it, the pure organic residue, we used as fertilizer or food for our mycoprotein.

I got used to staying up all night playing music with some of the other Wrong Headed kids, sometimes on the drum and sometimes on an old stringed instrument that was made of stained wood and had a leering cat face under its fret. Sometimes I thought I could hear something in the way our halting beats and scratchy notes bounced off the walls and the water beyond, like we were really conjuring a lost soundtrack. Sometimes it all just seemed like a waste.

What did it mean to be a real authentic person, in an era when everything great from the past was twenty feet underwater? Would you embrace prefab newness, or try to copy the images you can see from the handful of docs we'd scrounged from the Dataclysm? When we got tired of playing music, an hour before dawn, we would sit around arguing, and inevitably you got to that moment where you were looking straight into someone else's eyes and arguing about the past and whether the past could ever be on land or if it was doomed to be deep underwater forever.

I felt like I was just drunk all the time, on that cheap-ass vodka that everybody chugged in Fairbanks, or maybe on nitrous. My head was evaporating, but my heart just got more and more solid. I woke up every day on my bunk, or sometimes tangled up in someone else's arms and legs on the daybed, and felt actually jazzed to get up and go clean the scrubbers or churn the mycoprotein vats.

Every time we put down the bridge to the big island and turned off our moat, I felt everything go sour inside me, and my heart went funnel-shaped. People sometimes just wandered away from the Wrong Headed community without much in the way of good-bye—that was how Juya had gone—but meanwhile, new people showed up and got the exact same welcome that everyone had given to me. I got freaked out thinking of my perfect home being overrun by new selfish loud fuckers. Joconda had to sit me down, at the big table where sie did all the official business, and tell me to get over myself because change was the ocean and we lived by her mercy. "Seriously, Pris. I ever see that look on your face, I'm going to throw you into the myco vat myself." Joconda stared at me until I started laughing and promised to get with the program.

And then one day I was sitting at our big table, overlooking the straits between us and the big island. Staring at Sutro Tower and the tops of the skyscrapers poking out of the water here and there. And this obnoxious skinny bitch sat down next to me, chewing in my ear and talking about the impudence of impermanence or some similar. "Miranda," she introduced herself. "I just came up from Anaheim-Diego. Jeez, what a mess. They actually think they can build nanomechs and make it scalable. Whatta bunch of poutines."

"Stop chewing in my ear," I muttered. But then I found myself following her around everywhere she went.

Miranda was the one who convinced me to dive into the chasm of Fillmore Street in search of a souvenir from the old Church of John Coltrane, as a present for Joconda. I strapped on some goggles and a big apparatus that fed me oxygen while also helping me navigate a little bit, and then we went out in a dinghy that looked old enough to have actually been used for fishing. Miranda gave me one of her crooked grins and studied a wrinkled old map. "I thinnnnnk it's right around here." She laughed. "Either that or the Korean barbecue restaurant where the mayor got assassinated that one time. Not super clear which is which."

I gave her a murderous look and jumped into the water, letting myself fall into the street at the speed of water resistance. Those sunken buildings turned into doorways and windows facing me, but they stayed blurry as the bilge flowed around them. I could barely find my feet, let alone identify a building on sight. One of these places had been a restaurant, I was pretty sure. Ancient automobiles lurched back and forth, like maybe even their brakes had rusted away. I figured the Church of John Coltrane would have a spire like a saxophone? Maybe? But all the buildings looked exactly the same. I stumbled down the street, until I saw something that looked like a church, but it was a caved-in old McDonald's restaurant. Then I tripped over something, a downed pole or whatever, and my face mask cracked as I went down. The water was going down my throat, tasting like dirt, and my vision went all pale and wavy.

I almost just went under, but then I thought I could see a light up there, way above the street, and I kicked. I kicked and chopped and made myself float. I churned up there until I broke the surface. My arms were thrashing above the water and then I started to go back down, but Miranda had my neck and one shoulder. She hauled me up and out of the water and threw me into the dinghy. I was gasping and heaving up water, and she just sat and laughed at me.

"You managed to scavenge something after all." She pointed to something I'd clutched at on my way up out of the water: a rusted, barbed old piece of a car. "I'm sure Joconda will love it."

"Ugh," I said. "Fuck Old San Francisco. It's gross and corroded, and there's nothing left of whatever used to be cool. But, hey. I'm glad I found a group of people I would risk drowning in dead water for."

I chose to see that as a special status

Miranda had the kind of long-limbed, snaggle-toothed beauty that made you think she was born to make trouble. She loved to roughhouse and usually ended up with her elbow on the back of my neck as she pushed me onto the dry dirt. She loved to invent cute insulting nicknames for me, like "Dollypris" or "Pris Ridiculous." She never got tired of reminding me that I might be a ninth-level genderfreak, but I had all kinds of privilege, because I grew up in Fairbanks and never had to wonder how we were going to eat.

Miranda had this way of making me laugh even when the news got scary, when the government back in Fairbanks was trying to reestablish control over the whole West Coast, and extinction rose up like the shadows at the bottom of the sea. I would start to feel that scab inside my stomach, like the whole ugly unforgiving world could come down on us and our tiny island sanctuary at any moment; Miranda would suddenly start making up a weird dance or inventing a motto for a team of superhero mosquitos; and then I would be laughing so hard it was like I was squeezing the fear out of my insides. Her hands were a mass of scar tissue, but they were as gentle as dried-up blades of grass on my thighs.

Miranda had five other lovers, but I was the only one she made fun of. I chose to see that as a special status.

"What are you people even about?"

Falling in love with a community is always going to be more real than any love for a single human being could ever be. People will let you down, shatter your image of them, or try to melt down the wall between your self-image and theirs. People, one at a time, are too messy. Miranda was my hero and the lover I'd pretty much dreamed of since both puberties, but I also saved pieces of my heart for a bunch of other Wrong Headed people. I loved Joconda's totally random inspirations and perversions, like all the art projects sie started getting me to build out of scraps from the sunken city after I brought back that car piece from Fillmore Street. Zell was this hyperactive kid with wild half-braids, who had this whole theory about digging up buried hard drives full of music files from the digital age, so we could reconstruct the actual sounds of Marvin Gaye and the Jenga Priests. Weo used to sit with me and watch the sun going down over the islands, we didn't talk a lot except that Weo would suddenly whisper some weird beautiful notion about what it would be like to live at sea, one day when the sea was alive again. But it wasn't any individual, it was the whole group. We had gotten in a rhythm together, and we all believed the same stuff. The love of the ocean, and her resilience in the face of whatever we had done to her, and the power of silliness to make you believe in abundance again. Openness, and a kind of generosity that is the opposite of monogamy.

But then one day I looked up, and some of the faces were different again. A few of my favorite people in the community had bugged out without saying anything, and one or two of the newcomers started seriously getting on my nerves. One person, Mage, just had a nasty temper, going off at anyone who crossed hir path whenever xie was in one of those moods, and you could usually tell from the unruly condition of Mage's bleach-blond hair and the broke-toothed scowl. Mage became one of Miranda's lovers right off the bat, of course.

I was just sitting on my hands and biting my tongue, reminding myself that I always hated change and then I always got used to it after a little while. This would be fine: change was the ocean, and she took care of us.

Then we discovered the spoilage. We had been filtering the ocean water, removing toxic waste, filtering out excess gunk, and putting some of the organic by-products into our mycoprotein vats as a feedstock. But one day, we opened the biggest vat, and the stench was so powerful we all started to cry and retch, and we kept crying even after the puking stopped. Shit, that was half our food supply. It looked like our whole filtration system was off; there were remnants of buckystructures in the residue that we'd been feeding to our fungus, and the fungus was choking on them. Even the fungus that wasn't spoiled would have minimal protein yield. And this also meant that our filtration system wasn't doing anything to help clean the ocean, at all, because it was still letting the dead pieces of buckycrap through.

Joconda just stared at the mess and finally shook hir head and told us to bury it under the big hillside.

We didn't have enough food for the winter after that, so a bunch of us had to make the trip up north to Marin, by boat and on foot, to barter with some gun-crazy farmers in the hills. And they wanted free labor in exchange for food, so we left Weo and a few others behind to work in their fields. Trudging back down the hill, pulling the first batch of produce in a cart, I kept looking over my shoulder to see our friends staring after us, as we left them surrounded by old dudes with rifles.

I couldn't look at the community the same way after that. Joconda fell into a depression that made hir unable to speak or look anyone in the eye for days at a time, and we were all staring at the walls of our poorly repaired dormitory buildings, which looked as though a strong wind could bring them down. I kept remembering myself walking away from those farmers, the way I told Weo it would be fine, we'd be back before anyone knew anything, this would be a funny story later. I tried to imagine myself doing something different. Putting my foot down maybe, or saying fuck this, we don't leave our own behind. It didn't seem like something I would ever do, though. I had always been someone who went along with what everybody else wanted. My one big act of rebellion was coming here to Bernal Island, and I wouldn't have ever come if Juya hadn't already been coming.

Miranda saw me coming and walked the other way. That happened a couple of times. She and I were supposed to have a fancy evening together, I was going to give her a bath even if it used up half my water allowance, but she canceled. We were on a tiny island, but I kept only seeing her off in the distance, in a group of others, and whenever I got closer, she was gone. At last I saw her walking on the big hill, and I followed her up there, until we were almost at eye level with the Transamerica Pyramid coming up out of the flat water. She turned and grabbed at the collar of my shirt and part of my collarbone. "You gotta let me have my day," she hissed. "You can't be in my face all the time. Giving me that look. You need to get out of my face."

"You blame me," I said, "for Weo and the others. For what happened."

"I blame you for being a clingy wet blanket. Just leave me alone for a while. Jeez." And then I kept walking behind her, and she turned and made a gesture that connected with my chest, or else intentionally shoved me. I fell on my butt. I nearly tumbled head over heels down the rocky slope into the water, but then I got a handhold on a dead root.

"Oh, fuck. Are you okay?" Miranda reached down to help me up, but I shook her off. I trudged down the hill alone.

I kept replaying that moment in my head, when I wasn't replaying the moment when I walked away with a ton of food and left Weo and the others at gunpoint. I had thought that being here, on this island, meant that the only past that mattered was the grand, mysterious, rebellious history that was down there under the water, in the wreckage of San Francisco. All of the wild music submerged between its walls. I had thought my own personal past no longer mattered at all. Until suddenly, I had no mental energy for anything but replaying those two memories. Uglier each time around.

And then someone came up to me at lunch, as I sat and ate some of the proceeds from Weo's indenture: Kris or Jamie—I forget which. And he whispered, "I'm on your side." A few other people said the same thing later that day. They had my back, Miranda was a bitch, she had assaulted me. I saw other people hanging around Miranda and staring at me, talking in her ear, telling her that I was a problem and they were with her.

I felt like crying, except that I couldn't find enough moisture inside me. I didn't know what to say to the people who were on my side. I was too scared to speak. I wished Joconda would wake up and tell everybody to quit it, to just get back to work and play and stop fomenting.

The next day, I went to the dining area, sitting at the other end of the long table from Miranda and her group of supporters. Miranda stood up so fast she knocked her own food on the floor, and she shouted at Yozni, "Just leave me the fuck alone. I don't want you on 'my side,' or anybody else. There are no sides. This is none of your business. You people. You goddamn people. What are you people even about?" She got up and left, kicking the wall on her way out.

After that, everybody was on my side.

The honeymoon is over, but the marriage is just beginning

I rediscovered social media. I'd let my friendships with people back in Fairbanks and elsewhere run to seed, during all of this weird, but now I reconnected with people I hadn't talked to in a year or so. Everybody kept saying that Olympia had gotten really cool since I left, that there was a vibrant music scene now, and people were publishing zootbooks and having storytelling slams and stuff. And meanwhile, the government in Fairbanks had decided to cool it on trying to make the coast fall into line, though there was talk about some kind of loose articles of confederation at some point. Meanwhile, we'd even made some serious inroads against the warlords of Nevada.

I started looking around the dormitory buildings and kitchens and communal playspaces of Bernal, and at our ocean reclamation machines, as if I was trying to commit them to memory. One minute, I was looking at all of it as if this could be the last time I would see any of it, but then the next minute, I was just making peace with it so I could stay forever. I could just imagine how this moment could be the beginning of a new, more mature relationship with the Wrong Headed crew, where I wouldn't have any more illusions, but that would make my commitment even stronger.

I sat with Joconda and a few others, on that same stretch of shore where we'd all stood naked and launched candles, and we held hands after a while. Joconda smiled, and I felt like sie was coming back to us, so it was like the heart of our community was restored. "Decay is part of the process. Decay keeps the ocean warm." Today Joconda had wild hair with some bright colors in it and a single strand of beard. I nodded.

Instead of the guilt or fear or selfish anxiety that I had been so aware of having inside me, I felt a weird feeling of acceptance. We were strong. We would get through this. We were Wrong Headed.

I went out in a dinghy and sailed around the big island, went up toward the ruins of Telegraph. I sailed right past the Newsom Spire, watching its carbon-fiber cladding flake away like shiny confetti. The water looked so opaque, it was like sailing on milk. I sat there in the middle of the city, a few miles from anyone, and felt totally peaceful. I had a kick of guilt at being so selfish, going off on my own when the others could probably use another pair of hands. But then I decided it was okay. I needed this time to myself. It would make me a better member of the community.

When I got back to Bernal, I felt calmer than I had in ages, and I was able to look at all the others—even Mage, who still gave me the murder eye from time to time—with patience and love. They were all my people. I was lucky to be among them.

I had this beautiful moment, that night, standing by a big bonfire with the rest of the crew, half of us some level of naked, and everybody looked radiant and free. I started to hum to myself, and it turned into a song, one of the old songs that Zell had supposedly brought back from digital extinction. It had this chorus about the wild kids and the war dance and a bridge that doubled back on itself, and I had this feeling, like maybe the honeymoon is over, but the marriage is just beginning.

Then I found myself next to Miranda, who kicked at some embers with her boot. "I'm glad things calmed down," I whispered. "I didn't mean for everyone to get so crazy. We were all just on edge, and it was a bad time."

"Huh," Miranda said. "I noticed that you never told your peeps to cool it, even after I told the people defending me to shut their faces."

"Oh," I said. "But I actually," and then I didn't know what to say. I felt the feeling of helplessness, trapped in the grip of the past, coming back again. "I mean, I tried. I'm really sorry."

"Whatever," Miranda said. "I'm leaving soon. Probably going back to Anaheim-Diego. I heard they made some progress with the nanomechs after all."

"Oh." I looked into the fire, until my retinas were all blotchy. "I'll miss you."

"Whatever." Miranda slipped away. I tried to mourn her going, but then I realized I was just relieved. I wasn't going to be able to deal with her hanging around, like a bruise, when I was trying to move forward. With Miranda gone, I could maybe get back to feeling happy here.

Joconda came along when we went back up into Marin to get the rest of the food from those farmers and collect Weo and the two others we had left there. We climbed up the steep path from the water, and Joconda kept needing to rest. Close to the water, everything was the kind of salty and moist that I'd gotten used to, but after a few miles, everything got dry and dusty. By the time we got to the farm, we were thirsty, and we'd used up all our water, and the farmers saw us coming and got their rifles out.

Our friends had run away, the farmers said. Weo and the others. A few weeks earlier, and they didn't know where. They just ran off, left the work half done. So, too bad, we weren't going to get all the food we had been promised. Nothing personal, the lead farmer said. He had sunburnt cheeks, even though he wore a big straw hat. I watched Joconda's face pass through shock, anger, misery, and resignation, without a single word coming out. The farmers had their guns slung over their shoulders, enough of a threat without even needing to aim. We took the cart, half full of food instead of all the way full, back down the hill to our boat.

We never found out what actually happened to Weo and the others.

That's such an inappropriate line of inquiry I don't even know how to deal

I spent a few weeks pretending I was in it for the long haul on Bernal Island, after we got back from Marin. This was my home, I had formed an identity here that meant the world to me, and these people were my family. Of course I was staying.

Then one day, I realized I was just trying to make up my mind whether to go back to Olympia or all the way back to Fairbanks. In Fairbanks, they knew how to make thick-cut toast with egg smeared across it, and you could go out dancing in half a dozen different speakeasies that stayed open until dawn. I missed being in a real city, kind of. I realized I'd already decided to leave San Francisco a while ago, without ever consciously making the decision.

Everyone I had ever had a crush on I had hooked up with already. Some of them I still hooked up with sometimes, but it was nostalgia sex rather than anything else. I was actually happier sleeping alone, I didn't want anybody else's knees cramping my thighs in the middle of the night. I couldn't forgive the people who sided with Miranda against me, and I was even less able to forgive the people who sided with me against Miranda. I didn't like to dwell on stuff, but there were a lot of people I had obscure, unspoken grudges against, all around me. And then occasionally I would stand in a spot where I'd watched Weo sit and build a tiny raft out of sticks, and I would feel the anger rise up all over again. At myself, mostly.

I wondered about what Miranda was doing now and whether we would ever be able to face each other again. I had been so happy to see her go, but now I couldn't stop thinking about her.

The only time I even wondered about my decision was when I looked at the ocean and the traces of the dead city underneath it, the amazing heritage that we were carrying on here. Sometimes I stared into the waves for hours, trying to hear the soundwaves trapped in them, but then I started to feel like maybe the ocean had told me everything it was ever going to. The ocean always sang the same notes, it always passed over the same streets and came back with the same sad laughter. And staring down at the ocean only reminded me of how we'd thought we could help heal her, with our enzyme treatments, a little at a time. I couldn't see why I had ever believed in that fairy tale. The ocean was going to heal on her own, sooner or later, but in the meantime, we were just giving her meaningless therapy that made us feel better more than it actually helped. I got up every day and did my chores. I helped repair the walls and tend the gardens and stuff. But I felt like I was just turning wheels to keep a giant machine going, so that I would be able to keep turning the wheels tomorrow.

I looked down at my own body, at the loose kelp-and-hemp garments I'd started wearing since I'd moved here. I looked at my hands and forearms, which were thicker, callused, and more veiny with all the hard work I'd been doing here—but also, the thousands of rhinestones in my fingernails glittered in the sunlight, and I felt like I moved differently than I used to. Even with everything shitty that had happened, I'd learned something here, and wherever I went from now on, I would always be Wrong Headed.

I left without saying anything to anybody, the same way everyone else had.

A few years later, I had drinks with Miranda on that new floating platform that hovered over the wasteland of North America. Somehow we floated half a mile above the desert and the mountaintops—don't ask me how, but it was carbon neutral and all that good stuff. From up here, the hundreds of miles of parched earth looked like piles of gold.

"It's funny, right?" Miranda seemed to have guessed what I was thinking. "All that time, we were going on about the ocean and how it was our lover and our history and all that jazz. But look at that desert down there. It's all beautiful, too. It's another wounded environment, sure, but it's also a lovely fragment of the past. People sweated and died for that land, and maybe one day it'll come back. You know?" Miranda was, I guess, in her early thirties, and she looked amazing. She'd gotten the snaggle taken out of her teeth, and her hair was a perfect wave. She wore a crisp suit and she seemed powerful and relaxed. She'd become an important person in the world of nanomechs.

I stopped staring at Miranda and looked over the railing, down at the dunes. We'd made some pretty major progress at rooting out the warlords, but still nobody wanted to live there, in the vast majority of the continent. The desert was beautiful from up here, but maybe not so much up close.

"I heard Joconda killed hirself," Miranda said. "A while ago. Not because of anything in particular that had happened. Just the depression, it caught up with hir." She shook her head. "God. Sie was such an amazing leader. But, hey, the Wrong Headed community is twice the size it was when you and I lived there, and they expanded onto the big island. I even heard they got a seat at the table of the confederation talks. Sucks that Joconda won't see what sie built get that recognition."

I was still dressed like a Wrong Headed person, even after a few years. I had the loose flowy garments, the smudgy paint on my face that helped obscure my gender rather than serving as a guide to it, the straight-line thin eyebrows and sparkly earrings and nails. I hadn't lived on Bernal in years, but it was still a huge part of who I was. Miranda looked like this whole other person, and I didn't know whether to feel ashamed that I hadn't moved on, or contemptuous of her for selling out, or some combination. I didn't know anybody who dressed the way Miranda was dressed, because I was still in Olympia, where we were being radical artists.

I wanted to say something. An apology, or something sentimental about the amazing time we had shared, or I don't even know what. I didn't actually know what I wanted to say, and I had no words to put it into. So after a while I just raised my glass, and we toasted to Wrong Headedness. Miranda laughed, that same old wild laugh, as our glasses touched. Then we went back to staring down at the wasteland, trying to imagine how many generations it would take before something green came out of it.

NOTE

Acknowledgment: Thanks go to Burrito Justice for the San Francisco map I consulted and Terry Johnson for the biotech insight.

CONTRIBUTORS

Samira Ahmed was born in Bombay, India, and grew up in Batavia, Illinois, in a house that smelled like fried onions, spices, and potpourri. She currently resides in Chicago. She also lived in New York City and Kauai, where she spent a year searching for the perfect mango. A graduate of the University of Chicago, Samira has taught high school English, worked in education non-profits, and spent time on the road for political campaigns. Her creative non-fiction and poetry have appeared in *Jaggery Lit*, *Entropy*, the *Fem*, *Claudius Speaks*, *This Is What a Librarian Looks Like*, and the *Spine Out* novelists series. Her debut novel, *Love, Hate and Other Filters*, was an instant *New York Times* best seller. Her next two novels, *Internment* and *Mad, Bad and Dangerous to Know*, will both be out in 2019. Find her at https://samiraahmed.com or on Twitter or Instagram @sam_aye_ahm.

Charlie Jane Anders is the author of *All the Birds in the Sky* (2016), which won the Nebula, Locus, and Crawford Awards and was nominated for a Hugo Award. Her story "Six Months, Three Days" won a Hugo Award, and her novel *Choir Boy* (2005) won a Lambda Literary Award. Her short fiction has appeared in *Tin House*, *Conjunctions*, *Wired*, *Tor.com*, *Asimov's Science Fiction*, the *Magazine of Fantasy and Science Fiction*, and many other magazines and anthologies. She carries around a tiny red button in her pocket that will shut down the entire Internet, and she never presses it but thumbs it constantly.

Cynthia Arrieu-King is an associate professor of creative writing at Stockton University and a former Kundiman fellow. Her books include *People Are Tiny in Paintings of China* (2010) and *Manifest* (2013), winner of the Gatewood

Prize, selected by Harryette Mullen. She edited the "Asian Anglophone" edition of *Dusie* in 2016.

Cynthia Atkins is the author of *Psyche's Weathers* (2007), *In The Event of Full Disclosure* (2013), and a manuscript in progress, "Still-Life with God." Her work has appeared or is forthcoming in *Alaska Quarterly Review, Apogee Journal, Bomb, Cleaver Magazine, Del Sol Review, Diode, Entropy, Expound,* the *Florida Review, Green Mountains Review, North American Review, Seneca Review, Sweet: A Literary Confection, Tampa Review, Thrush, Tinderbox,* and *Verse Daily.* Her poems have been nominated for the Pushcart Prize, and she has received prizes and fellowships from Bread Loaf Writers' Conference and Writers at Work. She teaches creative writing at Blue Ridge Community College and lives on the Maury River in Rockbridge County, Virginia.

Herman Beavers is professor of English and Africana studies at the University of Pennsylvania, where he teaches courses in African American literature and creative writing. His books include a scholarly monograph, *Geography and the Political Imaginary in the Novels of Toni Morrison* (2018), and a chapbook, *Obsidian Blues* (2017).

Jericho Brown is the recipient of fellowships from the John Simon Guggenheim Foundation, the Radcliffe Institute for Advanced Study at Harvard University, and the National Endowment for the Arts. His poems have appeared in the *New York Times* and the *New Yorker.* His first book, *Please* (2008), won the American Book Award. His second book, *The New Testament* (2014), won the Anisfield-Wolf Book Award. He is an associate professor at Emory University.

Adrienne Celt is a writer and cartoonist living in Tucson, Arizona. She is the author of the novels *The Daughters* (which won the 2015 PEN Southwest Book Award) and *Invitation to a Bonfire* (2018). Her short fiction has appeared in the *O. Henry Prize Stories 2016, Esquire, Ecotone, Epoch, Prairie Schooner,* the *Kenyon Review,* and many other places, and her comics have been published by the *Rumpus,* the *Toast, Bat City Review,* and *Broad!* and on her longrunning webcomic *Love among the Lampreys* (http://loveamongthelampreys .com). She has also published a collection of her comics, *Apocalypse How? An Existential Bestiary* (2016).

Rene Denfeld is the best-selling author of *The Child Finder* (2017) and *The Enchanted* (2014). Her novels, inspired by her day job as an indigent defense investigator, have won numerous honors, including a French Prix du Premier

Roman Étranger, an ALA Excellence in Fiction Award. Her work has been long-listed for the Andrew Carnegie Medal for Excellence in Fiction and the IMPAC Dublin Literary Award. The *Enchanted* was a finalist for the Center for Fiction First Novel Prize. Rene has worked as the chief investigator for a public defenders office and has handled hundreds of cases over the years, exonerating innocents from prison and helping sex-trafficking victims. She is currently the Oregon Regional Arts and Culture Council literature fellow, using her position to address the rights of the dispossessed. She was awarded the Break the Silence Award in Washington, D.C., in 2017 in recognition for her justice work. Rene lives in Portland, Oregon, where she is the happy mother to three children she adopted from foster care.

Linh Dinh is the author of ten books, the latest a poetry collection, *A Mere Rica* (2017), and the nonfiction *Postcards from the End of America* (2017). He maintains a very active photo and political essay blog.

Veronica Scott Esposito is the author of four books, most recently *The Doubles* (2017). She is a frequent contributor to the *Times Literary Supplement* and the *San Francisco Chronicle*, and her work has appeared in *Tin House*, the *White Review*, the *Lifted Brow*, the *Believer*, the *Washington Post*, and others. She was a finalist for the 2014 Graywolf Nonfiction Prize.

Sarah Rose Etter is the author of *Tongue Party* (2011). Her work has appeared or is forthcoming in *Vice Magazine*, *Juked*, *Salt Hill Journal*, *Black Warrior Review*, and others. She is a contributing editor at the *Fanzine*, a columnist at *Philadelphia Weekly*, and a cofounder of the *Tire Fire* reading series. She has attended the Gullkistan creative residency in Iceland and presented work at the Society for the Study of American Women Writers conference in Bordeaux, France.

Melissa Febos is the author of the memoir *Whip Smart* (2010) and the essay collection *Abandon Me* (2017). Her work appears in *Tin House*, *Prairie Schooner*, *Granta*, the *Kenyon Review*, *Lenny Letter*, the *New York Times*, *Glamour*, *Vogue*, and elsewhere. The recipient of fellowships from the MacDowell Colony, Virginia Center for the Creative Arts, Vermont Studio Center, Ragdale, Lower Manhattan Cultural Council, and others, she is an assistant professor at Monmouth University and serves on the board of VIDA: Women in Literary Arts.

Stephanie Feldman is the author of the novel *The Angel of Losses* (2014), a Barnes and Noble Discover Great New Writers selection, winner of the

Crawford Award, and finalist for the Mythopoeic Award. Her short stories and essays have appeared in or are forthcoming from *Asimov's Science Fiction*, *Electric Literature*, the *Magazine of Fantasy and Science Fiction*, the *Maine Review*, the *Rumpus*, and *Vol. 1 Brooklyn*. She lives outside Philadelphia with her family.

Liana Finck is a cartoonist whose work appears regularly in the *New Yorker*, the *Awl*, and *Catapult* and on her Instagram feed. Her graphic novels include *A Bintel Brief* (2014) and *Light and Shadow*, forthcoming from Random House.

Ganzeer is an artist whose brand of cultural insurgency can be seen in museums and galleries across Europe, North Africa, South America, and the United States. His street art was integral to the creative surge associated with the Tahrir Square uprising, and his writing has appeared in *Das Magazin*, the *Cairo Review of Global Affairs*, and *Salon*. His latest work, a long in-progress sci-fi graphic novel, *The Solar Grid*, earned him a Global Thinker Forum Award from *Foreign Policy* in 2016. He has lived in Cairo, New York, Los Angeles, and now Denver, which to him feels like the quietest place on Earth.

Nancy Hightower has published fiction and creative nonfiction in *Sundog Lit*, *Word Riot*, the *Huffington Post*, *Entropy*, *Vol. 1 Brooklyn*, and elsewhere. She is the author of *The Acolyte* (2015) and *Elementari Rising* (2013) and from 2014 to 2016 was the science fiction and fantasy reviewer for the *Washington Post*. She is now working on a book about digital narratives with Paul D. Miller (a.k.a. DJ Spooky) and a memoir about growing up in the evangelical South.

Bassey Ikpi is a Nigerian American writer and mental health advocate. She is the founder of mental health organization the Siwe Project. Bassey is also a contributing editor for *Catapult*. Her debut memoir, *Making Friends with Giants*, is forthcoming from Harper Perennial.

Mohja Kahf has been a professor of comparative literature and Middle Eastern studies at the University of Arkansas since 1995. She is the author of the poetry books *E-mails from Scheherazad* (2003) and *Hagar Poems* (2016) and the novel *The Girl in the Tangerine Scarf* (2006).

Ken Kalfus is the author of three novels, *Equilateral* (2013), *The Commissariat of Enlightenment* (2003), and *A Disorder Peculiar to the Country* (2006), which was a finalist for the 2006 National Book Award. He has also published three collections of stories, *Thirst* (1998); *Pu-239 and Other Russian Fantasies* (1999), a finalist for the PEN/Faulkner Award; and *Coup de Foudre: A Novella and Stories* (2015). A film adaptation of his short story "Pu-239" aired on HBO in 2007.

Joy Ladin, Gottesman Professor of English at Yeshiva University, is the author of seven books of poetry, including Lambda Literary Award finalists *Impersonation* (2015) and *Transmigration* (2009) and two new collections, *Fireworks in the Graveyard* (2017) and *The Future Is Trying to Tell Us Something: New and Selected Poems* (2017). Her memoir of gender transition, *Through the Door of Life*, was a 2012 National Jewish Book Award finalist. Her work has been recognized with a National Endowment for the Arts fellowship and a Fulbright scholarship, among other honors. A new work of creative nonfiction, *I Am What I Will Be: Reading God and the Torah from a Transgender Perspective*, is forthcoming from Brandeis University Press.

Ana-Maurine Lara, Ph.D., is a national award-winning poet and fiction writer. She is author of the fiction works *Erzulie's Skirt* (2006), *Cuando el sol volvió a cantar al pueblo* (When the sun once again sang to the people; 2011), and *Watermarks and Tree Rings* (2013) and the poetry book *Kohnjehr Woman* (2017). In 2015, she completed the first of her decade-long projects, *Cantos*. Ana-Maurine is a Cave Canem fellow and is an assistant professor at the University of Oregon.

Carmen Maria Machado is the author of the short story collection *Her Body and Other Parties* (2017), which was a finalist for the National Book Award, the Kirkus Prize, and the National Book Critics Circle's John Leonard Prize and the winner of the Bard Fiction Prize. Her memoir *House in Indiana* is forthcoming from Graywolf Press, and her work has appeared in the *New Yorker*, *Granta*, *Tin House*, *Guernica*, *Gulf Coast*, *NPR*, *Best American Science Fiction and Fantasy*, and elsewhere. She is the writer in residence at the University of Pennsylvania and lives in Philadelphia with her wife.

Juan Martinez is the author of the short story collection *Best Worst American* (2017). His work has appeared in *Glimmer Train*, *Huizache*, *McSweeney's*, *Ecotone*, National Public Radio's *Selected Shorts*, and elsewhere. He lives in Chicago with his family and can be found online at http://www.fulmerford .com.

Airea D. Matthews is the author of the poetry collection *Simulacra* (2017) and recipient of the 2016 Yale Series of Younger Poets prize. Her work has appeared in the *Rumpus, Best American Poetry 2015, American Poets*, and elsewhere. She received the 2016 Rona Jaffe Foundation Writers' Award and was awarded the Louis Untermeyer Scholarship in 2016 from Bread Loaf Writers' Conference. Airea is working on her second poetry collection, "Under/class," which explores poverty. She is an assistant professor at Bryn Mawr College.

Diane McKinney-Whetstone is the author of six novels, including the best-selling *Tumbling* (1996) and, most recently, *Lazaretto* (2016). She was twice awarded the Black Caucus of the American Library Association Literary Award for fiction. She lives in Philadelphia—the city she mines for her material—and is at work on her seventh novel.

Lynn Melnick is the author of the poetry collections *Landscape with Sex and Violence* (2017) and *If I Should Say I Have Hope* (2012). Her poetry has appeared in *APR*, the *New Republic*, the *New Yorker*, the *Paris Review*, *A Public Space*, and elsewhere, and she has written essays and book reviews for *Boston Review*, the *Los Angeles Review of Books*, and *Poetry Daily*, among others. A 2017–2018 fellow at the New York Public Library's Cullman Center for Scholars and Writers, she also teaches poetry at the 92Y and serves on the executive board of VIDA: Women in Literary Arts.

Sam J. Miller is a writer and a community organizer. His stories have been nominated for the Nebula, World Fantasy, and Theodore Sturgeon Awards and have appeared in over a dozen "year's best" anthologies. He is a graduate of the Clarion Science Fiction and Fantasy Writers Workshop and a winner of the Shirley Jackson Award. His debut novel, *The Art of Starving* (2017), was one of NPR's Best Books of 2017 and was followed by *Blackfish City*, forthcoming from Ecco Press. He lives in New York City and at http://samjmiller.com.

Liz Moore is the author of the novels *The Words of Every Song* (2007), *Heft* (2012), and *The Unseen World* (2016). Her short fiction and creative nonfiction have appeared in such venues as *Tin House*, the *New York Times*, and *Narrative Magazine*. A winner of the 2014 Rome Prize in Literature, Liz lives in Philadelphia, where she is writer in residence in Temple University's MFA program in creative writing.

Eileen Myles is a poet, novelist, and art journalist and author of twenty books, most recently *Afterglow* (2017). Eileen lives in New York City and Marfa, Texas.

Sandra Newman is the author of seven books, most recently a novel, *The Country of Ice Cream Star* (2014), which was long-listed for the Folio Prize and the Baileys Women's Prize for Fiction. She has written two other novels (the first, *The Only Good Thing Anyone Has Ever Done* [2002], was short-listed for the Guardian First Book Award) and four works of nonfiction, including (with Howard Mittelmark) *How Not to Write a Novel* (2008).

Alice Notley has published over forty books of poetry, including (most recently) *Benediction* (2015), *Negativity's Kiss* (2013), and *Certain Magical Acts* (2016). She has received many awards, including the Academy of American Poets' Lenore Marshall Prize, the Poetry Society of America's Shelley Award, the Griffin International Prize, two National Endowment for the Arts grants, the *Los Angeles Times* Book Prize for poetry, and the Ruth Lilly Poetry Prize. She lives and writes in Paris, France.

Cynthia Dewi Oka is a poet and the author of *Salvage* (2017) and *Nomad of Salt and Hard Water* (2016). A three-time Pushcart Prize nominee, her poems have appeared in *American Poetry Review*, the *Kenyon Review*, *Guernica*, the *Massachusetts Review*, *Black Renaissance Noire*, *Painted Bride Quarterly*, and elsewhere. Her work appears in *Best of Kweli* (2017) and *Women of Resistance: Poems for a New Feminism* (2018), among other anthologies. She has received the *Fifth Wednesday Journal* Editor's Prize in Poetry, scholarships from Voices of Our Nations (VONA) and the Vermont Studio Center, and the Leeway Foundation Transformation Award. Originally from Indonesia, she currently works as an organizer with immigrant communities in Philadelphia.

Tahneer Oksman is an assistant professor of academic writing at Marymount Manhattan College. Her work has appeared in the *Los Angeles Review of Books*, the *Comics Journal*, the *Forward*, *Public Books*, the *Guardian*, *Lilith*, and *Cleaver Magazine*, for which she is the graphic narrative reviews editor. Her first book, a work of literary criticism, is *"How Come Boys Get to Keep Their Noses?" Women and Jewish American Identity in Contemporary Graphic Memoirs* (2016). Currently, she is writing a book exploring memoirs about absence, loss, and grief.

Malka Older is a writer, aid worker, and Ph.D. candidate. Her science fiction political thriller *Infomocracy* was named one of the best books of 2016 by *Kirkus Reviews*, *Book Riot*, and the *Washington Post*, and has two sequels, *Null States* (2017) and *State Tectonics* (forthcoming from Macmillan). Named Senior Fellow for Technology and Risk at the Carnegie Council for Ethics in International Affairs for 2015, she has more than a decade of experience in humanitarian aid and development. Her doctoral work on the sociology of organizations at the Institut d'Études Politiques de Paris (Sciences Po) explores the dynamics of multilevel governance and disaster response using the cases of Hurricane Katrina and the Japan tsunami of 2011.

Craig Santos Perez is a native Chamorro from the Pacific Island of Guam. He is the author of four books, most recently *From Unincorporated Territory [Lukao]* (2017). He is an associate professor in the English Department at the University of Hawaii, Mānoa, where he teaches Pacific literature, creative writing, and ecopoetry.

Nathaniel Popkin is the author of three books of nonfiction, including *Philadelphia: Finding the Hidden City* (2017), and two novels, *Lion and Leopard* (2013) and *Everything Is Borrowed* (2018). His work has appeared in the *Wall Street Journal, Tablet,* the *Kenyon Review, Rain Taxi, Public Books, Lit Hub,* the *Rumpus,* and the *Millions.*

Marc Anthony Richardson received his master of fine arts degree from Mills College. He is an artist and writer from Philadelphia. *Year of the Rat,* his debut novel, was the winner of the 2015 Ronald Sukenick Innovative Fiction Prize. In 2017, it received an American Book Award from the Before Columbus Foundation, founded by Ishmael Reed. He also was the recipient of a Zora Neale Hurston/Richard Wright fellowship and a Vermont Studio Center residency. Currently, he is writing "The Messiahs," a work of speculative fiction that takes place in a possible America where you can take on the capital punishment of a relative, a derivative of the Native American blood law.

Carlos José Pérez Sámano is a literary fiction and nonfiction author and a teacher of creative writing workshops in Mexico, the United States, Kenya, and Cuba. He has four published books in Spanish and is the recipient of the Ad Zurdum Publishing House's Best Seller award. His work has been featured in more than twenty international magazines, including *Fredericksburg Literary and Art Review, Errr Magazine, Quinqué, Poetry in Common,* and *Cultura Colectiva.* He is pursuing a master of fine arts in creative writing and a master's in publishing at Rosemont College. Find him on Twitter @carlosjoseperez.

Jeffrey Stockbridge is a photographer living and working in Philadelphia. Photographing predominantly with a large-format film camera, he documents the elusive underbelly of inner-city life. His photographs have been exhibited at the National Portrait Gallery in London, the Philadelphia Museum of Art, the Delaware Art Museum, and the Delaware Center for the Contemporary Arts. Jeffrey has received numerous grants and awards, including a Pennsylvania Council on the Arts grant, an Independence Foundation Fellowship grant, and a Center for Emerging Visual Artists Fellowship. His first book, *Kensington Blues*, was released in 2017.

Madeleine Thien was born in Vancouver, the daughter of Malaysian-Chinese immigrants to Canada. Her most recent novel, *Do Not Say We Have Nothing*, about art, music, and revolution in twentieth-century China, won the 2016 Scotiabank Giller Prize and the 2016 Governor General's Literary Award for fiction and was short-listed for the Man Booker Prize, the Baileys Women's Prize for Fiction, and the Folio Prize. Her four books have been translated into more than twenty-five languages. She is professor of English at Brooklyn College.

Edwin Torres came to poetry through performance art in New York City's East Village in the early 1990s. His books include *Xoeteox: The Infinite Word Object* (forthcoming from Wave Books), *Ameriscopia* (2014), *Yes Thing No Thing* (2010), and *The PoPedology of An Ambient Language* (2007). His work appears in several anthologies, including *American Poets in the 21st Century: The New Poetics*, vol. 2; *Angels of the Americlypse: An Anthology of New Latin@ Writing*; *Postmodern American Poetry*, vol. 2; and *Aloud: Voices from the Nuyorican Poets Cafe*.

KC Trommer is the author of the chapbook *The Hasp Tongue* (2014). A graduate of the MFA program at the University of Michigan, Ann Arbor, KC has been the recipient of an Academy of American Poets Prize. Her poem "Fear Not, Mary" won the 2015 *Fugue* poetry prize and was nominated for a Pushcart Prize. In 2017, the Grammy Award–winning composer Herschel Garfein created the song cycle "Three Rides" for soprano, cello, and piano from her work. She lives in Jackson Heights, Queens, with her son.

Adam Vines is an associate professor of English at the University of Alabama at Birmingham, where he is editor of *Birmingham Poetry Review* and director of the English Honors Program. He has published poems in *Poetry*, the *Kenyon Review*, *Southwest Review*, *Measure*, *Gulf Coast*, the *Hopkins Review*, and *Subtropics*, among others. He is the author of *Out of Speech* (2018) and *The Coal Life* (2012) and coauthor of *Day Kink* (2018) and *According to Discretion* (2015).

Fran Wilde is the author of several novels and short stories that have been nominated for Nebula Awards and Hugo Awards, including her Andre Norton Award– and Compton Crook Award–winning debut novel, *Updraft* (2015); its sequels, *Cloudbound* (2016) and *Horizon* (2017); and the novelette *The Jewel and Her Lapidary* (2016). Her short stories appear in *Asimov's Science Fiction*, *Tor.com*, *Beneath Ceaseless Skies*, *Shimmer*, *Nature*, and the 2017 *Year's Best Dark Fantasy and Horror*. She writes for publications including the *Washington Post*, *Clarkesworld Magazine*, *io9*, and *GeekMom*. You can find her on Twitter, on Facebook, and at http://www.franwilde.net.